BLIND LOYALTY

101 LOYALTY CONCEPTS RADICALLY SIMPLIFIED

AMANDA CROMHOUT

INTERNATIONAL LOYALTY PERSONALITY OF THE YEAR

To my Thee, Han, KK, and Joshie –
I couldn't have done this without you!

Blind Loyalty's author: Amanda Cromhout

Paula Thomas, Founder and CEO Let's Talk Loyalty:
Amanda Cromhout is one of the people I feel most lucky to have met throughout my career. Instantly impressive, Amanda inspires trust in everyone who meets her, with a list of professional and athletic achievements that put most of us to shame. But it was her reaction to a recent incredibly painful experience, losing her sight in one eye, that showed Amanda's true power. Despite the trauma and challenges on her road to recovery, Amanda found ways to appreciate the blessings in her life and share them with others. Her story will inspire you to do the same.

Bruce Whitfield, South Africa's leading business journalist, author, and broadcaster:
"If you want loyalty, get a dog," said someone in the days long before people like Amanda Cromhout dreamed up new and creative ways of ensuring that you not only retain your customer, but build a deep and mutually beneficial relationship with them over a sustained period of time. Customer acquisition is one of the most time consuming and difficult aspects of running any business. Retaining them – and keeping them active – is vital. Amanda's deep understanding of loyalty programmes globally puts her at the nexus of some of the most creative and successful offerings in the world. This book provides a window into a world that to most of us is as complex as it is confounding. No customer is loyal because they like you. They are loyal because of the value proposition you offer, but it is no longer

good enough to simply give people what they want, where and when they want it – that is a basic requirement. This book will help you think differently about how best to engage your customer and keep them hooked.

Amanda Cromhout is Founder and CEO of an international loyalty consultancy Truth, based in Cape Town, South Africa. She is The International Loyalty Awards – *Loyalty Personality of the Year, 2023*. Established judge on international awards panels, she needs little or no introduction to the loyalty profession.

Amanda started her career as a graduate at British Airways and quickly immersed herself in the world of loyalty via The Executive Club and the oneworld global alliance. After 11 years at the airline, she joined Woolworths, South Africa's premier retailer as Executive Head of Customer. In 2010, she started Truth, a niche loyalty consultancy that today serves the world from the tip of Africa. Truth has worked with the best loyalty brands globally and is focused on loyalty consultancy and loyalty training. Amanda herself is the Academic Director of the Truth Customer Academy and runs coaching and mentorship programmes for loyalty professionals around the world.

Amanda is also passionate about giving back. Amongst other charitable activities, she is the Founder of The Blind Loyalty Trust, established after a life-changing condition that left her temporarily blind in one eye.

She lives life to the maximum; as an endurance athlete, she runs ultra marathons and Ironman events for fun. She completes the circle of life with her husband, Theo, and three amazing children.

www.amandacromhout.com

Blind loyalty, as defined in various dictionaries, has negative connotations like loyalty despite knowing better, implying some level of idiocy. Potentially – and controversially – I prefer to think of blind loyalty as that absolute level of loyalty beyond all other measures.

I started researching additional inspiration for this book when I was in the depths of my recent illness and I came across this quote:

> “ A loyalty programme is corrective eye surgery for business. — Rory Sutherland, Vice Chairman Ogilvy

It smacked me right between the eyes – excuse the pun. I was literally breathless because of its absolute relevance for the loyalty story I wished to express in *Blind Loyalty* and for the timing of my own corrective-eye surgery (or rather eye-saving surgery). Rory, you may never know this but your quotation had a more profound impact than you could have ever imagined.

Contents

Page 53 Section 2. Programme design and loyalty communications

Page 179 Section 4. Launching and managing a programme

Page 211 Section 5. Concluding thoughts

Blind Loyalty
Introduction

I have wanted to write a book about loyalty for a while now, but just couldn't find the right angle to differentiate it in any way. In 2022, I was struck by a terrifying eye condition which left me blind in my right eye and in extreme pain for three months. Ironically, the vision for writing Blind Loyalty came to me there and then, out of my blindness.

Everything in life needs simplifying. I have committed to writing this book to radically simplify the complexity of loyalty. At Truth, we work tirelessly at simplifying everything for our clients and they say they love our unpretentious and direct approach. We are in an age where very few have the attention span of more than a swipe of a social media page. So, the idea of two pages per concept – simple and compelling – means even the most distracted may wish to demystify a loyalty concept or two.

I wrote this book but I often refer to 'we' throughout referring to the work we do collectively for our clients at Truth. Blind Loyalty walks you through five sections: 1. strategy and data; 2. loyalty programme design; 3. industry excellence; 4. launching and managing a loyalty programme; and 5. concluding thoughts.

All profits generated through Blind Loyalty will go directly to The Blind Loyalty Trust, to help others who may endure the same terrifying condition as I did in 2022 but be unable to afford the required healthcare to save their eye. (See page 230.)

Acknowledgements

Nothing great is accomplished alone.
— Usman Mustafa

While I am not claiming any level of greatness in *Blind Loyalty*, I am certainly acknowledging the team of amazing humans who helped me bring this book to the loyalty world.

Firstly, to the team working on the book itself behind the scenes: my Dad, Brian Ryles, you made editing more fun than I could imagine. To the remarkable Truth team, who make coming to work every day simply phenomenal and who pulled out every stop possible to bring *Blind Loyalty* to life – thank you, especially to Lauren Venter, Rowen Gloyne, and Hannah Cromhout. Finally from a book production point of view, thank you to Caryn Gootkin, I learned so much from you; and to Claire Gunn, for your talent behind your camera and the front-cover shot. Joag van Rooyen (Africa Press), you were a gem to work with to pull off the publishing deadline so miraculously! Thank you.

I am so grateful to the many loyalty professionals who officially contributed to this book; you added incredible insight from your area of loyalty expertise. A full list of *Blind Loyalty* contributors is found on page 228. I'd also like to thank my good friend Paula Thomas for providing inspiration and resource to thousands of loyalty professionals via her podcast, *Let's Talk Loyalty*. It has helped enormously to sprinkle magic from your show throughout this book as factual and relevant examples to bring concepts alive.

I have been privileged to enjoy my career from the very first day at British Airways, back in 1994. I have one life-long mentor whom I still cherish for my career, but more importantly as a very close friend. Yossi Schwartz, thank you for everything over the many years.

Finally, and of course not least, I couldn't do any of this exciting loyalty work without the unwavering support of my beautiful family: my husband, Theo, and our remarkable children, Hannah, Katie, and Josh. Thank you all for letting me hide in my office to work passionately on things I love. A special mention to Theo for his creativity in the name *Blind Loyalty*, not only for this book but for The Blind Loyalty Trust.

An additional mention goes to ***fusarium keratitis***, defined by Google as "a severe ocular infection and a common cause of monocular blindness in the tropical and subtropical areas of the world". Affectionately known as the 'F' word by my eye surgeon, this F word created unprecedented havoc for my family and me and continues to have its impact. But, without its presence in 2022, *Blind Loyalty* may have remained a mere idea and never become a reality.

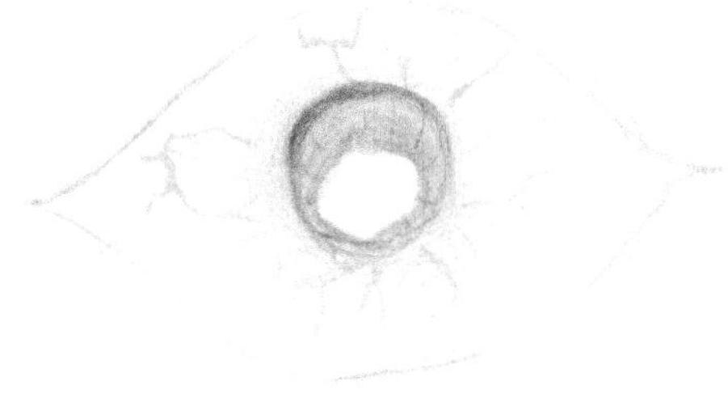

Illustration by Katie Cromhout

101 Loyalty concepts radically simplified

Section 1

Strategy and data

Chapter 1

Customer focus: is it even a question?

It fascinates me that questions are still being raised about investment into customer strategies. Companies are still inward focused rather than customer obsessed. Customers only want to spend their hard-earned disposable income with brands that truly want their business. Brands can show that they truly want to retain and delight their customers in any number of ways, which we will discuss throughout this book.

This book is about loyalty – customer loyalty or loyalty programmes. They are not the same and we cover this later, but it is staggering to hear the debates that continue to headline corporate board agendas regarding customer investment and trade offs to acquire customer data. Data legislation terrifies most executives and so it should. 'If in doubt, don't do it' should be the globally accepted mantra regarding responsible behaviour around customer data.

Unfortunately, too many decisions are made around short-term results from campaigns or seasons rather than longer term strategic focus on customer lifetime value. Companies become obsessed with acquiring new customers via deep incentives to lure them closer, whilst existing customers are enticed to continue to spend more or branch into categories which they may not wish to explore. None of this is new but it is, disappointingly, still too prominent in execution strategies. These are not customer focused; they are simply focused on short-term internal goals and KPIs.

Obviously, loyalty and CRM professionals around the world know that there is value in knowing who their customers are and how they shop, bank, and eat with you. This puts the power in the brands' hands to offer the most appropriate brand experience across all marketing channels and all choices facing your customers.

Customers are not stupid – quite the opposite, I'd say – they recognise that there is a value exchange for any level of data or data insight which they allow the brand to tap into. This value exchange could be in the form of loyalty and rewards, relevant offers, or simply better service or recognition. So brands must not expect the golden nugget of customer data or customer insight without deep reflection on what they are willing to offer in return in this value exchange.

> **Loyalty cannot be bought or created; it is earned as a result of loving, understanding and engaging with your customers on a level far deeper than even your greatest discount.**

Some companies feel obliged to create a loyalty programme for their members purely to fulfil the company focus on customer-centricity. This is a debateable motivation as some of the world's best brands do not have traditional loyalty programmes: think Apple and Coca Cola (although the latter certainly entertains loyalty tactics like points and rewards).

Chapter 2

The loyalty industry is not just child's play

If ever there was an industry explosion, it is in the loyalty sector. From tier one global brands through to the mom-and-pop coffee shop next door, everyone is doing it! Can they all be wrong? There has to be some sense in it somewhere for consumers and brands the world over to be committed to such a marketing force.

I sit around numerous boardroom tables with strong, experienced board members shaking their heads and saying, "I don't use loyalty programmes; are they really worth all this nonsense?" We remind the boardroom audiences that they are a sample of one and that loyalty usage in most markets is on the rise. In a market like South Africa, we consistently see statistics like 70–80% of the population use loyalty programmes.[1] What other marketing initiative yields such high response rates? That's just it: loyalty is not a marketing initiative if taken seriously by the brand. It is a strategic, company-wide approach to drive increased customer loyalty.

So, if every brand has a loyalty programme, how do they find space to differentiate? It is critical to address this, else having a loyalty programme within your marketing mix simply becomes another marketing 101 basic requirement. If all the brand does with its loyalty programme is launch it and acquire members without investing in the real magic, which we explain throughout this book, then it's a superfluous and impossibly expensive investment.

Back to the numbers: globally we see advanced marketing territories like the UK, Australia, and the USA boasting equally strong statistics as the South African consumer usage volumes. More than three quarters of Brits[2] have a loyalty card and almost 90% of Australians belong to one or more loyalty programmes. These numbers are huge. Americans are members of approximately 30 loyalty programmes[3] but this is tending to lead to less commitment to one or the other programme and loyalty promiscuity. Nevertheless, these numbers are undeniably on the rise. Such statistics show consumer behaviour towards loyalty programmes rather than the business commitment.

> **Over $300 billion investment globally in such an industry is not child's play.**

The size of commitment to the loyalty industry is insanely impressive i.e. loyalty operators themselves are investing deeply. Global research has yielded gargantuan numbers like over $300 billion financial commitment to the loyalty industry across loyalty and engagement platforms, loyalty rewards back to consumers, and internal investments in headcount to execute against the stated CRM and loyalty strategies.[4]

In addition, let's look at one of the oldest loyalty industries: airlines. The Frequent Flyer Programme (FFP) industry is quoted as a multi-billion dollar game. Some of the top US airlines' loyalty programmes are evaluated to be worth considerably more than Nasdaq market capitalisation values of the entire airline. For example, AAdvantage is seemingly worth more than double the market cap of American Airlines itself.[5]

Chapter 3

Evolution not revolution: the history of loyalty programmes

The history books show that loyalty programmes date back as far as Ancient Egypt when 'beer and bread' tokens were exchanged for items over and above simply beer and bread. Thereafter, the first traceable loyalty system is in 1793 with an American retailer issuing copper coins for redemption off future purchases. More well known, S&H Green Shield stamps were being issued by Sperry & Hutchinson trading company from 1896. In 1964, this developed into the S&H Green Shield catalogue. Every 50+ year-old marketing professional remembers their parents getting excited when their Green Shield stamp books filled up and were ready for redemption. My memory is slightly different but along the same lines. I remember my dad collecting stamps from the Shell garage and redeeming a full stamp card for a set of beer or Coca Cola glasses. Fast forward 40 years and my kids remember us shifting our fuel convenience shop spend from a competitor to the local Engen fuel convenience store to fill up stamps to collect fluffy puppies once the stamp card was full.

Interestingly, the legacy of the S&H Green Shield company continues. In Japan, the Green Stamp loyalty company is a thriving loyalty organisation. Founded in 1961, it creates the coalition offering for 23,000 retail stores, serving over 17 million Japanese consumers.

In 1929, Betty Crocker, a grocery retailing brand and a well-known fictional character in food and recipe campaigns, became the first known 'on pack' loyalty incentive via box-top cut-out coupons.

As early as 1966, we see the start of customer segmentation when American Express offers its highest value business travellers gold cards to differentiate their value to the Amex brand.

The next major milestone in loyalty history is that of Frequent Flyer Programmes (affectionately known as FFPs to the airline industry). American Airlines (AA) launched its AAdvantage programme in 1981. As discussed in the previous chapter, the FFP industry is said to be worth many billion dollars.

1983 sees the emergence of what we know as the first hotel rewards programme from Holiday Inn. Today, it is virtually impossible to stay at a multi-property hotel brand which doesn't have a loyalty programme.

Retail loyalty programmes have been in operation for centuries but the card-swipe loyalty system was most notably first mastered by Tesco in the UK, with its ClubCard, initially trialed in 1994 with its partner Dunnhumby. Before this, Tesco used Green Shield stamps as its promotional tool but was unable to gather any customer insight on transactional spend.

We've even seen a Netflix documentary about Pepsi Cola's incentive programme to collect 'Pepsi stuff', including the tongue-in-cheek incentive of a harrier jet in 1995.

The rest is history! Throughout this book, we continue to track progress in the loyalty industry via the adoption of technologies and advanced customer experience approaches.

Chapter 4

Customer loyalty or loyalty programmes

It is stating the obvious to say that customer loyalty and loyalty programmes are not the same, but they are way too often confused in marketers' minds. We often engage in discussions with loyalty operators who say they want a loyalty programme because they want customer loyalty. But we tell them a few points and prizes don't make long-term customer loyalty. It's not that easy.

What is customer loyalty? It can be defined as any number of things but the pivotal ingredient is trust. A company must invest so much more to build any form of trust.

> **Trust is the cornerstone of all things loyalty, gained through transparency and integrity.**

Trust is critical in all relationships, personal or professional, and loyalty is no different. For example, if you are clearly indicating to a brand through your transactional behaviour that you prefer vegan food options, you may be offended if offered barbeque specials for the finest Japanese Wagyu steak. This is a basic premise: brands must understand their customers and embark upon a journey of personalisation through communications, experiences, and broader brand promise.

It is also critical to listen to how customers respond to any questions you ask them. Upon registration into loyalty programmes, so many brands make the mistake of asking lifestyle questions and other ad hoc data requests. For example, 'what sports do you like?' if you are a sports retailer or 'what fashion choices do you prefer?' by clothing retailers. Nine times out of ten, such tick box responses are thereafter ignored apart from generic emailers targeted at male fashion consumers or female fashion consumers. Rather understand what consumers really want to hear from you based on their buying behaviours. We advise against data-gathering questionnaires at registration. They rarely do more than irritate the customer because brands simply don't listen to the responses.

Simple golden rule: if you don't know how to act upon or do not intend to act upon data received, do not ask for it. It erodes trust before the brand has even moved beyond its 'first date' stage.

Back to customer loyalty: it can be created and maintained if elements of your customer experience send the right signals to your consumers at the right times in a manner which makes sense for them and not simply to tick the boxes of the brand communications plan. Prioritise an outside-in (what is right for the customer) over an inside-out (what is right for the brand) approach.

Chapter 5

10Ps of loyalty marketing: the icing on the cake

Have you ever considered the importance of all the separate ingredients for a cake? If you miss one essential ingredient, what would happen to that delicious carrot cake? Loyalty programmes within your marketing mix are quite similar.

The ingredients of a cake recipe are like the 7Ps of product and service marketing. Let's unpack them. We start with 101 on Kotler's 4Ps of product, price, promotion and place. Anyone who has studied this knows that these create the foundation of a great offering. Is the product or service competitive? Is it offered at a price suitable to the market and offering? How is it promoted, advertised, communicated and what are the awareness levels? Finally, is it distributed (place) at a suitable location for consumers to buy or use it? In addition, we must mix in the additional 3Ps of service marketing, which are defined as people, physical evidence, and process. Are the people behind the brand a credit to the brand, adding value to the service experience? Does physical evidence resonate throughout the service experience and is it consistent? Finally, how easy is the brand to do business with (i.e. the process) or is it complex and lacking seamlessness whether online, instore or over the phone?

So what has this got to do with a cake? These 7Ps of product and service marketing are essential to the brand experience. A loyalty programme is the icing on the cake; the cake tastes yummier with icing on it. To remain competitive, consumers expect icing on all cakes these days, and the icing (aka loyalty programme) becomes the glue which ties the brand promise together (just like icing on a cake keeps the cake ingredients intact).

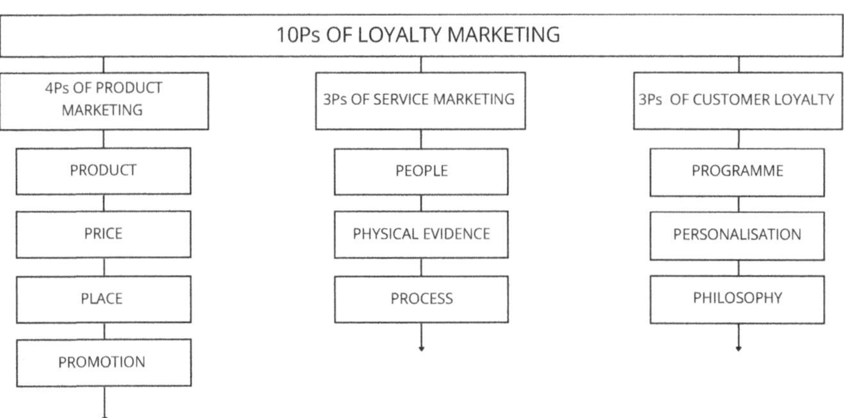

Truth Loyalty Marketing 10Ps

We call this icing on the cake the 3Ps of customer loyalty, programme, personalisation, and philosophy, making 10Ps overall. I think the programme element of the loyalty 3Ps is obvious, either a loyalty or a CRM programme; personalisation is the critical experience members or consumers have due to the programme being relevant; and, finally, philosophy means that the programme enables the brand to get across the philosophical ethos of the company through all communications and programme mechanics.

Chapter 6

CRM: it's not just a tech solution

CRM is probably the most misunderstood term in the marketing industry. Simply, the acronym stands for Customer Relationship Management. Depending on the task through which an organisation desires to better serve its customers, CRM may translate as simple call centre processes to check that service and product delivery are to standard. For other organisations, it may mean a more sophisticated and automated sales cycle, leading to increased customer acquisitions and ongoing sales performance per customer. So, in order to define exactly what CRM is, we need to start with what it isn't.

CRM is not simply the 'tech solution', although many may argue that it is. If you google CRM's definition, responses include that CRM is the tech solution to help you manage customer data. While many organisations need an automated CRM technical capability to properly manage their database, follow through on required sales processes, and automate communications, all of this can be achieved through a number of technical solutions or one all-encompassing technical capability that delivers all customer-related requirements.

To better understand what Customer Relationship Management means for an organisation, answer these questions:

1. Strategically, what do you wish to achieve through better customer management?
2. How do you collect customer data and what permissions do you have?
3. How do you wish to communicate to your customer base? This will include frequency, segments, and channel.
4. How automated do you wish the communications to be?
5. How deeply do you wish to nurture customer relationships over and above the communication process? This may include the requirement to build a loyalty or incentivisation scheme.

Only once you can articulate responses to these types of questions can you define the best CRM approach for your brand. And only then can the type of technical requirement be defined. This is why CRM itself is not only the 'tech solution' but its delivery will require a CRM technical capability integrated into the rest of your business architecture.

> **Customer relationship management (CRM) is a process in which a business or other organisation administers its interactions with customers, typically using data analysis to study large amounts of information.**
> **— ScienceDirect[6]**

Chapter 7

Customer experience: everything communicates!

Customer experience, often shortened to CX, is another widely used but often misunderstood customer term. It encompasses much more than customer service or customer loyalty. Think of your all time favourite brand: what are the component parts that make up the positive experience? How does it make you feel?

CX starts before purchase or service delivery. It starts at the consideration stage, when the consumer researches product, price, testimonials, and the like. Customers will experience the product or service during an engagement, either over time or in the moment of transaction. What happens after the transaction will also have an impact on customer's experience of the brand. All interactions with the brand, staff at a store or in a call centre, the website, and digital channels (social media) will impact customer experience. All communications received will impact customer experience, be they marketing push (e.g. weekly newsletter or promotional SMS) or operational communications (e.g. transaction confirmation post purchase). Finally, how consistently the brand is managed and promoted will impact how customers experience the brand. As I said … everything communicates!

One of the most powerful ways to improve customer experience is to remove all friction points so the customer enjoys a seamless process. Less friction will also make management of the process easier and more efficient for the brand itself.

There are industry approved approaches to measure customer experience. Probably the most well known and used is Net Promotor Score (NPS), developed by Fred Reichheld from Bain & Company in 2003. Quite simply, customers are asked one question: "How likely are you to recommend this product or company?" The responses are measured from 0 (lowest) to 10 (highest). Responses yield results of how many or what percentage of customers are 'Detractors', 'Passives', and 'Promoters'. Detractors score 0 to 6, Passives 7 or 8, and Promoters 9 or 10.

Another much less widely used methodology for customer experience measurement is CSAT: customer satisfaction score. Broadly speaking, such a measure is achieved by surveying customers and asking: "How satisfied were you with this product or company?"

> **Brands that have a superior customer experience bring in 5.7 times more revenue than their competitors. — Forbes[7]**

To identify a standout brand in customer experience, I referred to the 2022 winner of the International Loyalty Awards: Best Customer Experience. The winner was everest Bite Club from Greece. "Bite Club is a real competitive advantage for the company. Very good use of data, excellent management of customer journeys". It was also singled out for creativity and functionality behind its design, as well as the "innovative gamification mechanisms that fully meet customer expectations."[8]

Chapter 8

The greatest of them all: customer centricity

The ultimate goal for brands should be customer centricity, which requires long-term investment from management. Anything less than C-suite buy-in will not yield customer centricity to its fullest.

Customer centricity is so much more than customer experience, customer loyalty, or customer service. It becomes an obsessive culture informing every decision made within the organisation - from annual planning cycles and staffing decisions through to product or service delivery. No investment in systems or product development is considered unless it adds to the customer-centric approach of the organisation.

Customer centricity requires a change in strategy, culture, structure, processes, and a customer plan. It begins with an understanding and ability to drive customer-led insights to guide the business.

> **Customer-centric companies live and breathe their customers and are laser focused on providing amazing experiences. — Forbes[9]**

Many chapters in this book will speak to customer data and insight but I'd like to use an example taken from my retail days of how Tesco used its ClubCard loyalty data to drive customer-led business decisions rather than relying purely on product- or category-led data.

According to Tesco's representatives on the conference circuit at the time, the ClubCard data enabled an obscure but powerful decision for the biscuit category that would not otherwise have been taken. The Hobnobs biscuit brand saw its tubular encased biscuits (that had significantly lower sales volumes – five times fewer sales per week) staying on the shelf instead of a higher volume product: cellophane wrapped biscuits. Why? Surely sales data would keep the larger sales performing product on the shelf? However, on using deeper customer insight over and above product sales performance, Tesco realised that the more expensive, tubular wrapped product was purchased by its most valuable customer segment and on nine out of ten trips to the store. Customer data for the less expensive, cellophane wrapped biscuits revealed that its customers were placed in less valuable customer segments and only occasionally purchased the product, at a rate of approximately four out of ten trips to the store. Based on this customer insight, the tubular wrapped Hobnobs product retained its shelf space in the biscuit aisle.

The question organisations should ask is: what is your 'Hobnob' analysis? Which decisions would you make differently if you reviewed business performance from a customer perspective rather than traditional product- or organisational-centric approaches? The Hobnob example is one of thousands of daily business decisions which could improve results if approached from an angle of dedicated customer centricity.

Chapter 9

Culture eats strategy for breakfast

'Culture eats strategy for breakfast' – an overused statement that rings louder and louder each time I come across the impact of culture and senior management commitment on customer centricity and loyalty. The success of such strategies depends on whether the culture of the organisation is fully aligned to operate in a customer-centric manner and whether the leaders buy in to drive this approach. Unfortunately, I have witnessed too many amazingly talented marketing executives start customer initiatives that don't drive real change due to lack of understanding, support, and drive from senior leaders. We are always so relieved and it always makes for a more exciting and successful project when customer strategies are initiated at CEO or managing director level.

One of my fondest customer projects is a perfect example of this. I worked with a premium retailer that collected significant customer data but in disparate silos across the business. Tasked with driving customer strategy, we created the single view of the customer and incredibly powerful segmentation models to offer insight and actionable strategies for the business to implement. The reaction from the broader business was one of intrigue and curiosity. However, no real buy-in was achieved until the CEO stood up and confirmed his support for a customer-led approach in which decision making and investment needed to be completed through a customer lens. Years and deep silos of retail experience are not easily challenged...

> **This took time. The CEO certainly wasn't on board initially.**

In fact, therein lies the opportunity and challenge. Using customer insight to become customer centric is not to change the way a business operates but to supplement and to challenge it. Eighty percent of insight from customer data will back up what businesses should already know about their customers and performance. The remaining 20% is where the magic happens. Aided by new insight, executives start to challenge some forever-old assumptions.

The principle of 'you don't know what you don't know' very much applies to the change management process of bringing customer insight into a changing customer-centric environment. Change management is at the heart of a successful customer-centric transformation and some basic change management principles will go a long way to help the success of customer centricity:

- Create a test and trial plan using customer insight to deliver a series of proof of concept initiatives.
- Over communicate.
- Overly simplify the insight so the most hurried executive can easily understand the point of differentiation being communicated.
- Find customer champions to help drive the story within their division. They can help celebrate successes and find test and trial ideas to initiate change in their department.
- Over communicate.
- Ensure every piece of customer insight is headlined with a simple 'So what?' statement like, 'So what am I going to do differently now that I know this?'
- Did I say over communicate?!

To the converted, customer centricity makes complete sense. To the masses, however, it is a tough organisational shift, which requires change management and senior love of the project.

Chapter 10

Customer-centric businesses

Sometimes, the only way to effectively define customer centricity is to showcase some leading examples where brands are excelling.

Nordstrom, a North American fashion and general merchandise retailer, has been trading for over a century. It operates a loyalty programme called The Nordy Club, which is a simple programme: earn points on transactional spend plus exclusive member-only perks. Nordstrom operates a customer-first business where its staff are acknowledged for going the extra mile for customers. It is obsessively focused on customer experience across its various channels: store, website, app. This includes simple touches like a customer-friendly returns policy. Jason Mestrits, a senior executive at Nordstrom, openly outlines a methodical data strategy and how a data-driven operation sits beneath Nordstrom's success.[10]

Amazon combines the science and soul of retailing. Starting with the customer and working backwards. Data is at the core of the entire business operation to optimise marketing strategies and link buyers and sellers through Amazon's publishing platform. Machine learning is used to continuously improve every element of its core operations, little by little: "True innovation is not an invention but an improvement," says Jeff Bezos.

> I want Amazon to be the most customer-centric organisation on earth.
> — Jeff Bezos, Executive Chairman Amazon

Bank of Queensland: Fondly know as BOQ, Australian-based Bank of Queensland really stands out in its focus on building strong customer relationships. Its mission is to prove that "it's possible to love a bank". This required a reinvention of its approach for lending and associated digital, streamlined and automated processes. Customer satisfaction scores soared and time for processing applications was dramatically reduced.

Some organisations adopt a customer charter as a foundation to their approach to customer centricity. Extracted below is Doug Leather's view of a customer charter. Doug was an incredibly respected industry colleague and friend who sadly departed this world very prematurely but, thankfully, left us with his book *The Customer Centric Blueprint*, 2013, which is an incredible read.

> A customer charter is a tool used by some companies to define this overall proposition to the customer. Companies such as NatWest, Royal Bank of Scotland and AAMI (an Australian insurer) are using customer charters to define the standards of service that customers expect. In AAMI's case, their customer charter is extremely audited, annually reviewed, and the results are publically reported. There are eight promises made and AAMI incurs a penalty in the terms of the charter that have been breached. This demonstrates true leadership and commitment to their overarching proposition 'to always provide its customers with the highest standards of customer service'.

Chapter 11

Customer insight: diamond in the rough

Working your way through customer data can feel like searching for a diamond in the rough. I use the analogy of a diamond because when you find the insight, it's worth the hunt.

As soon as an organisation embarks upon its journey of customer strategy and gathering customer data, it will have more data than it really knows what to do with. This is when it is critical to keep searching for insight rather than just data.

As described earlier in the book, the critical principle is that each piece of customer data should only be used and communicated within the business if there is a powerful 'so what?' question headlining each powerpoint slide bursting with customer data. What does this mean practically? For example, if the business is trying to illustrate the insight from the Tesco Hobnob case study (in Chapter 8), it should not present data trended over time of different products within the category and across different segments. Rather highlight the insight, i.e. that the more expensive but lower volume product is very unlikely to be substituted by your most valuable customers. Given that the frequency of purchase was 90% of transactions, the insight should highlight this business risk if the product were to substituted in the biscuit category planning cycle.

I always discuss with the data scientists in companies embarking on customer strategy that they must let the data do the talking. Allow the data to lead the 'investigation' to find the diamond in the rough. It is a balance of push and pull. Data scientists looking for the diamond may or may not find it in the row on row of customer data. But, whilst doing so, another precious stone of customer insight may present itself when least expected. The very best data minds I have worked with are perpetually curious and never rest. They deliberately go 'off brief' – and must be encouraged to do so – to find the precious insights within the structured customer data.

There is a famous quote in the world of customer loyalty, eminating from the early years of customer data during the Tesco ClubCard trial, initiated and managed by Dunnhumby, a global leader in customer data. This work changed the retail loyalty landscape across the globe forever. Tesco's Chairman at the time, Lord MacLaurin praises Dunnhumby's customer insight and the many diamonds in the rough which traditional retailers would not have been exposed to about their own customers.

> **"What scares me about this is that you know more about my customers after three months than I know after 30 years.**
> **— Lord MacLaurin, Tesco's Chairman (1994)**

Chapter 12

Unknown to known: getting to know your customers

One of the most obvious reasons brands decide to launch a loyalty programme is to entice customers to identify themselves. This is particularly relevant in the bricks and mortar retail environment. Online retail stores already know who is transacting with them but it is not always that simple in a physical store. Other industries like financial services, whether that be retail banking or insurance, for example, have an easier task of identifying customers. To do business with financial services companies, it's virtually always a pre-requisite to have registered via formal identification before any transaction can take place.

For the retail industry, the identification of customers in store and their associated shopping behaviours is the silver thread to customer centricity and understanding your customers better to ultimately serve them better.

Naively, many retail organisations want customers to sign up and thereafter to identify themselves at the point of sale (POS), even if they don't have a formal loyalty programme. Customers are savvy and are very unlikely to sign up for anything unless there is a fair value exchange. Organisations need to make it obvious why they are collecting data of any sorts. Customers need to immediately understand the benefits of a card swipe or a cellphone number entered at POS. A formal loyalty programme is the most obvious way to incentivise customers to identify themselves but this needs financial and organisational commitment. Unfortunately, companies try shortcuts via short-term incentives that are often neither sustainable, nor attractive to customers.

> **As you're planning or re-evaluating your first party data strategy, an important question to ask is: 'Have we made it easy for customers to see the benefits of sharing their data with us?' — Think with Google[11]**

KYC (know your customer) strategies are abound in organisations but remember that customers may not wish to be known or give out their personal information.

When we researched this in the *Truth and BrandMapp Loyalty Whitepaper*,[12] there was not a clear-cut response. Almost 30% of consumers responded that they feel brands should not use personal data at all, whilst the same number responded that it's acceptable as long as it results in better deals for them (i.e. a fair value exchange). A further 28% of consumers responded that it's fine as long as you know brands are doing it. There must, therefore, be transparency and trust as the backbone of the data exchange relationship between brands and consumers.

Chapter 13

Not all customers are created equal

One of the most powerful aha moments executives experience from the first set of customer insights when starting on their customer journey is that they simply don't have to treat all customers equally. Customers behave differently; they spend more or less and at vastly different frequencies, which results in different conclusions regarding customer value and profitability.

Applying the Pareto Principle, also known as the 80/20 rule, to marketing means that 20% of your customer base will give you 80% of your business value. In reality, we tend to see this equate to 20% of customers yielding approximately 75% of total revenue or turnover. More acutely, customer-spend distribution curves show that your highest spending 3% of customers will yield 20% of your revenue. These statistics mean that the remaining 80% of customers are contributing only 25% of your total turnover.

This immediately highlights some major flaws in most marketing budget allocations. Many brands have curated a sizeable database of customers but until they understand this powerful distribution curve of customers versus revenue contribution, they won't know which customers are most valuable versus customers with minimal or no value to the business. If the current marketing plan is to communicate weekly promotions via SMS to the entire customer base, we can quickly assess the enormous cost of this approach. A database of 1 million customers, for example, would cost approximately $12,000 per week. This is a sizeable $624,000 pa for a weekly promotional SMS communication.

Given that the top 20% of customers are more engaged in the brand and that 75% of turnover comes from this group of customers, careful thought needs to be given to how many of the remaining 80% of customers should receive the weekly SMS.

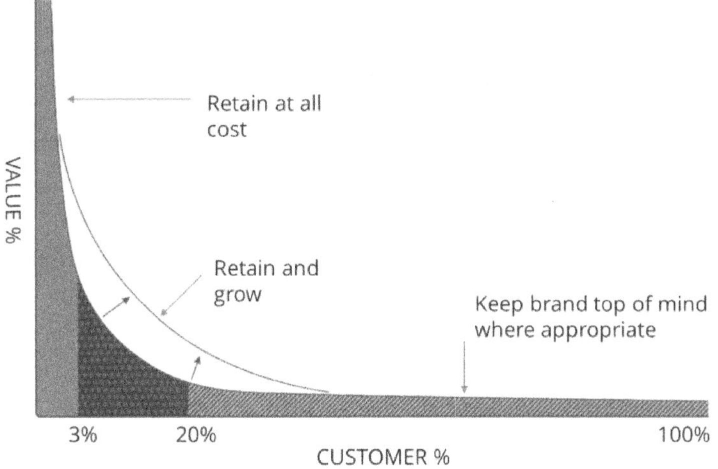

Customer and value distribution curve

There is no question that there is still value in communicating to some customers sitting in the 'long tail' of customer distribution, but knowing which customers is key. Deeper analysis is required to conclude which of the 80% will change behaviour and offer some return on investment. Which customers will be re-activated to start spending again? Which customers will be enticed to make one more purchase?

Chapter 14

At the end of every data point is a human

Contribution to this chapter is taken from an interview I did with Dr Shorful Islam, the CEO of Be Data Solutions, on the Let's Talk Loyalty podcast show.[13] Shorful holds a doctorate in psychology and is fascinated with how data represents human behaviour.

❝ —— Contribution by Shorful Islam

From a psychology point of view, you're actually looking at data points and trying to map and predict behaviours, and then also infer intent. I see data as a representation of human behaviour.

We look at the different types of customer groups and ultimately predict what they're going to do and how customers are going to respond, which will make sure that loyalty programmes are more successful. For example, we review which segment we should try to get a higher share of wallet. My 'secret sauce' really is about understanding that groups or segments of customers don't see themselves as one homogenous group.

Most importantly, don't forget that at the end of the loyalty programme, i.e. at the end of the data point, is a human. One of the dangers is that we leave everything to AI: artificial intelligence. A lot of AI really relies purely on historical behaviour. This means that you're using historical data to always predict what you do and how you're going to be optimising solutions for the 'past me', not the 'future me'. This is where humans come in to operate the machines which use AI. It can't all be left to AI, data and machines. We need humans to manage the data which represents humans: i.e. people and customers.

”

Shorful's discussion regarding AI was debated at the Comarch User Group loyalty conference in Paris in September 2022. Rather than AI meaning artificial intelligence, it was suggested that it should be called 'augmented intelligence'. Layering human input on top of automated crunching of lines of data results in augmented intelligence, i.e. the human input augments the output of artificial intelligence alone.

A report from Forrester[14] shows that the investments which companies claim have contributed the most to understanding their customers and customer needs is as follows:-

56% Customer analytics
52% Customer data management
49% Marketing automation

There is no question that companies are focusing their investment decisions into customer data infrastructure, analytics and execution. However, delivering a customer data capability is not simple and not without hurdles. As quoted below from the Harvard Business Review,[15] what seems simple can become the most challenging to deliver upon.

The biggest gaps in real-time customer analytics capabilities are in the areas of accessing customer data, performing analytics on that data, and taking action based on the resulting insights. — Harvard Business Review

Chapter 15

Death of the cookie: long live first party data!

Not so long ago terminology like first party data didn't enter our marketing vocabulary. Now, first party and zero party data KPIs become marketers' daily targets and strategic imperatives. What is driving this?

Fortunately for the loyalty and CRM community, there has been a global focus on consumer privacy legislation, which we cover in the next chapter. This is good for consumers and good for businesses. This has stretched beyond CRM and direct marketing and is also laser focused on the digital marketing and commerce environments.

'Death of the cookie' means that consumers may no longer be tracked online by third party cookies. Safari and Firefox have already blocked third party cookies and Chrome promises to do the same by 2024. This means that marketers will no longer be allowed to access individualised browsing habits of consumers. There will be aggregated data available but individual consumers are protected.

Ultimately, this changes the media investment decisions and effectiveness of online media spend. Media spend in social channels like Facebook will be less effective. Consumer preferences and attitudes towards online advertising are changing quite dramatically as consumers become more aware of data privacy legislation and consumer rights.

> **Seventy-nine percent of consumers would like it if brands spent less on Facebook advertising and invested more into their own loyalty programmes to reward consumers for their business. — Cheetah Digital[16]**

The 'death of the cookie' has accelerated focus on brands investing more heavily into their data acquisition strategies, which is good news for the CRM and loyalty industry. Budgets are starting to shift with less resistance than before and less competition from traditional media.

For simplicity, let's define some terms:

Third party data, for example, job title or credit rating, is provided by a third party. It is not always clear how they sourced the data (possibly through scraping or partnerships).

Second party data, for example, social media profile, is collected with the user's consent but via a partner (i.e. not directly).

First party data, for example, email address or cellphone number, is collected with user's consent via a transaction or sign-up to a mailing list.

Zero party data, for example, interests and communication preferences, is collected with consent, directly from the user, who is willing to share information over and above simple contact details.

Chapter 16

Data legislation: good for consumers and good for business

It's no longer the wild west! Thank goodness global markets have tightened legislation regarding use of personal information. Data legislation in Europe is governed by GDPR: General Protection Data Regulation, which came into effect in 2018. In the USA there is a more fragmented approach with different regulations governing different industries and different types of data, so it is more challenging to identify one over-arching privacy law to call upon. POPIA or the Protection of Personal Information Act came into effect in South Africa in 2020. Another significant loyalty market, Australia, sees its data governed by the Australian Privacy Act (1988), which seems aligned to principles set out in GDPR. We could go on, listing act upon act, country upon country.

One of the biggest human rights challenges in the 21st century after climate change is probably the violation of data privacy.
— De Stadler, Hattingh, Esselaar & Boast[17]

Data legislation is a complex subject feared by loyalty marketers. Hopefully, the simple definitions in this chapter will aid understanding and mitigate fear.

This extract,[18] taken from the key principles of GDPR, sets out principles that companies must comply with to fulfil most data protection requirements.

Lawfulness, fairness and transparency: lawful and fair processing of personal data is required. It must be transparent to consumers what data is being collected, used, and processed about themselves.

Purpose limitation: data should only be collected for the purpose explicitly explained at the point of collection.

Data minimisation: the data should only be processed for the minimal purpose for which it was collected.

Accuracy: data must remain accurate and up to date. Any inaccurate data is to be erased.

Storage limitation: time limits must be set against the purpose of why the data is collected. After such time limits, personal data should be destroyed.

Integrity and confidentiality: appropriate channels and technical structures need to be implemented to ensure the security and confidentiality of data collected are protected.

Accountability: companies need to prove accountability and compliance to over-arching data legislation, via appropriate records and measures.

Chapter 17

Why do loyalty at all?

By now this may seem like the craziest question of them all. It is, however, an extremely significant question.

Implementing a loyalty programme is not always the right solution unless you can strategically answer why you wish to create it and how it will aid in achieving your broader business objectives. We have certainly worked with brands who initially start out with the intention of designing and implementing a loyalty programme, but after deeper investigation and reflection have concluded that this is not necessary and alternative customer solutions, like a tailored CRM plan, will actually better serve their objectives.

Nevertheless, there are a number of reasons why it makes sense to forge ahead. We usually like to assess this against these six discussion points below:

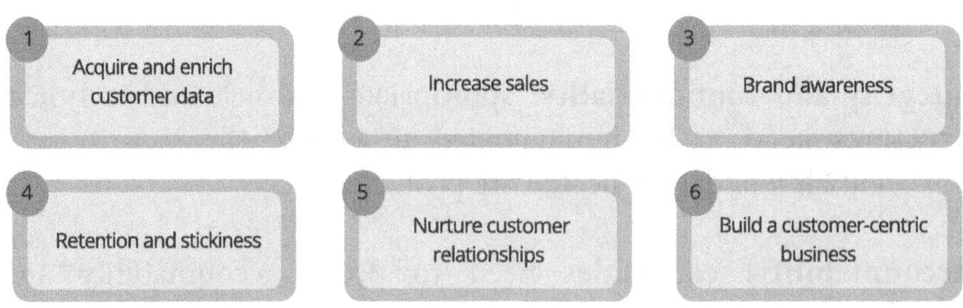

Why do loyalty? Six discussion points

We have thoroughly reflected in earlier chapters on the need for customer data, which is our very first strategic question.

Next, businesses need to reflect on whether the loyalty programme is required to help increase sales, profit or customer lifetime value. Without question, we have seen a change in revenue from engaged loyalty programme members. This is often a 4–6% increase in revenue. Some global practitioners work to over 10% incrementality, but I prefer to be more conservative based on experience. In research, consumers also state that they will switch their shopping, banking, fuel purchase behaviours, and so on if enticed to do so via a compelling loyalty proposition. In fact, the MIT Sloan Management Review found that "members of top-performing loyalty programmes are significantly more likely to intend to increase their spend."

> **Consumers who participate in top-quartile loyalty programmes are 91% more likely to intend to increase their spend.**
> **— MIT Sloan Management Review[19]**

Although brand awareness, our third question, is the least likely to be impacted by a loyalty programme, undoubtedly loyalty can have a role. However, typically marketers spend most of their time and budget worrying about brand awareness.

Retention is without question a key output of a well implemented loyalty programme and we dedicate the pages it deserves later in this book (see chapter 98).

Questions five and six, i.e. nurturing customer relationships and customer centricity, are key objectives that businesses aim to achieve via loyalty programmes. Earlier chapters discuss how loyalty programmes help businesses gather customer data and use insight gained from analysing the data to change their entire approach from a product- or supplier-led organisation to a customer-centric business.

Chapter 18

Loyalty promiscuity

Is it even possible to be loyal to a brand? We can start to answer this question by first evaluating human nature and then assess the loyalty statistics.

Loyalty is defined as "the quality of staying firm in your friendship or support for someone or something."[20] Much of loyalty and faithfulness is driven through emotional connection.

Throughout this book, we will talk about emotional loyalty. The impact in loyalty terms is greater if the customer feels an emotional connection to the brand because of or maybe regardless of the loyalty brand (see chapter 96).

Zelda la Grange ©™ @ZeldalaGrangeSA
I'm on so many rewards programmes, I think I even get points when I walk. Hopefully I'll 1 day qualify on a program for a free trip to George

This amusing tweet from Zelda la Grange (former Private Secretary to Nelson Mandela) perhaps epitomises how many customers feel about the loyalty brands they have signed up for.

The smartest loyalty-minded customers are not the most promiscuous. To generate maximum personal return from loyalty engagement, customers need to choose their preferred brands and stick to them. We are frequently asked: "How can consumers maximise their loyalty programmes?" It's simple! Which are customers' preferred brands to use regardless of loyalty programme? Consolidate your spend across multiple merchants in the same category and focus on one programme to gain maximum rewards. The customer must deeply understand that loyalty programme to ensure all benefits are maximised. If the customer is open to switching which brand they use in a certain category, then the better loyalty programme for their spend levels will sway the decision. If customers don't consolidate spend and use multiple programmes, they may find such promiscuity leads to lower overall reward levels.

Promiscuous

[pruh-mis-kyoo-uhs]
- adjective

1. Characterised by or involving indiscriminate mingling or association.[21]

All too often we see promiscuity amongst loyalty partners, which leads to a higher cost of sale for the partnering brand. The most effective partnerships are strategic and meaningful. Some brands seem to partner with way too many other brands – i.e. 'indiscriminate mingling' as per the definition above. This can be confusing for customers who don't understand which brands work with which loyalty programmes and will compromise commercial loyalty performance for partners and the loyalty brand.

Chapter 19

The Iceberg Effect

The beauty and complexity of loyalty programmes is that one size certainly does not fit all. There is often a customer value proposition at the centre of the loyalty offering that is available to everyone to participate in, understand, and rise through the tiers (if tiered and if goals are achieved). This will be well communicated as the core loyalty programme set of benefits and we refer to this as the overt loyalty proposition.

OVERT

LOYALTY PROPOSITION:

Available to everyone who may wish to join the programme or who is 'eligible' to participate in the programme

COVERT

CRM PERSONALISATION:

Personalised approach using strategic segments achieved through data segmentation

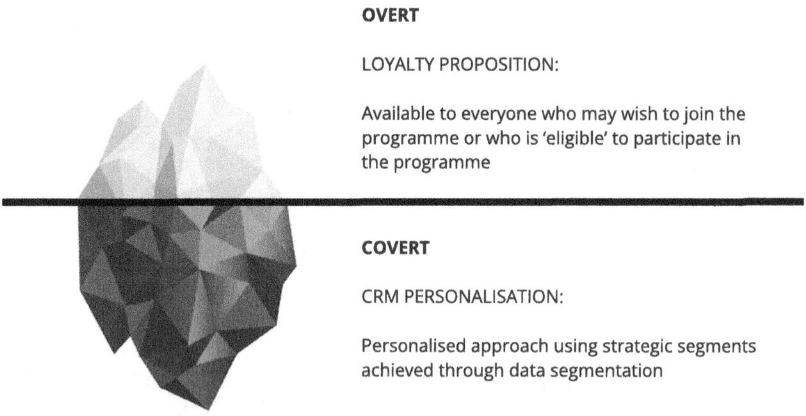

The Iceberg Effect

Loyalty programmes typically use overt propositions to attract new members to join the programme and actively engage in a data exchange or enrolment exercise. However, the real magic in terms of adding most value to customers and creating positive behavioural change takes place when the covert proposition is activated.

What do we mean by a covert proposition? It is not available to all members who enrol and will be personalised based on data gathered from programme participation. Consider chapter 13, where the distribution of customers against value shows in the simplest of forms how customers are not all the same based on behavioural measures, let alone stated preferences. Chapter 13 highlights, for example, how the top 3% of customers in terms of customer value represent a sales contribution of approximately 20%. The next 17% of customers in terms of value represent a contribution of 55% of sales.

Knowing this should drive loyalty operators to follow the simplest of covert strategies in treating the top 3% and top 20% of customers with a bespoke proposition that drives a deeper loyalty experience for these identified members.

What could this look like? A surprise-and-delight strategy would add enormous value to how customers perceive the brand and engender deeper emotional connections. Potentially, the top 3% of customers could be invited to an exclusive 'money-can't-buy' experience, either associated with the brand or not if it still adds value in a way customers will appreciate. The next 17% of customers could receive a deeper and more meaningful birthday offering from the loyalty programme or a sneak peak of pre-release new seasonal editions. We unpack the endless potential of surprise-and-delight strategies in chapter 51.

In conclusion, the Iceberg Effect builds the appropriate loyalty programme strategy to attract new members and be meaningful for most through its overt proposition, combined with adding real differentiated value to the most loyal customers in its covert proposition.

Section 2

Programme design and loyalty communications

Chapter 20

Loyalty programme structures

Understanding how loyalty programmes are structured is potentially one of the most confusing starting points for new loyalty managers. We are exposed to so many programmes in our own lives, but pinpointing how certain structures differ from others and for what reason or benefit to the customer and operating brand, is not simple. This chapter aims to offer the simplest starting point.

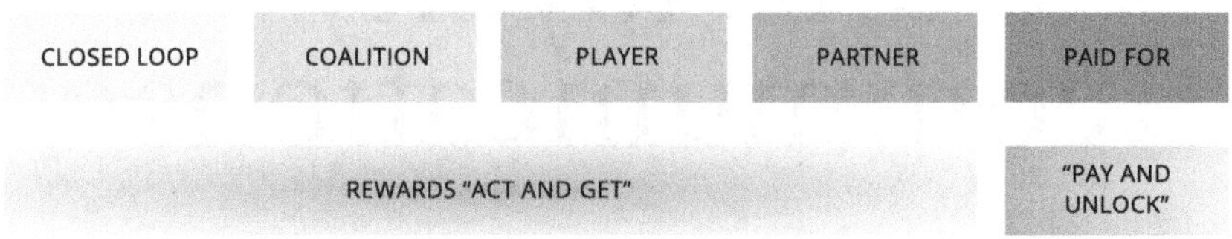

Loyalty programme structural options

Closed loop: Many loyalty programmes start as a closed-loop programme and evolve over time into more sophisticated structures. A closed-loop programme offers ways to earn rewards and redeem opportunities in the operating brand only. A classic example of a closed-loop programme is a coffee shop, where you can earn stamps or points for coffee and food purchases and the only place you can redeem these stamps or points is back in that same coffee shop. There are no partners. A South African coffee brand, Vida e Caffè, is a wonderful example of a popular closed-loop programme.

Coalition loyalty programmes are well established across the globe but have recently come under the scrutiny of many in the industry. Principally, a coalition programme is a multi-partner programme operated by a loyalty programme brand and which members join to earn and redeem their points across multiple merchants (often non-competing). This is explained in detail in chapter 22.

Player refers to a brand playing in another company's loyalty programme. The world of loyalty programme partnerships is promiscuous as we know from chapter 18, so we see some brands operating their own programme and playing in other company's programmes. It can get quite complicated, to say the least. Retail banking loyalty brands often operate their loyalty programmes with numerous other brands playing in their programme. They are not operating a coalition programme per se, as the principal existence of the bank's loyalty brand is to service the bank and its banking customers. It is more of a hybrid version of coalition, partner and player.

Partner is often used for any two or more brands that collaborate for the benefit of the customer and themselves. We discuss this in more detail in chapter 23, however, for simplicity, we define it here as two or more complementary brands that join together to add value for customers and the companies operating them. Classic examples are airlines' frequent flyer programmes offering interchangeability with car rental reward currencies and hotel loyalty benefits. They all operate in the same travel ecosystem.

Finally, **subscription** or paid-for loyalty models have a firm place in the customers' repertoire of brands to choose from. There is an animated debate around whether subscription models are really loyalty programmes or a paid-for service and we unwrap this in more detail in chapter 24.

Chapter 21

Closed loop – simple, simple, simple

The simplest of all loyalty programme structures is the closed loop. Typically, this is where many loyalty programmes start their loyalty offering to their customers. Naturally, over time, however, additional partners and complexities are added and programmes evolve. Many programmes that start as closed-loop systems slowly but surely move away from pure closed-loop structures.

The definition of a closed-loop loyalty programme is simply a programme involving only one company. Points and rewards are exchanged exclusively within the brand or its subsidiary brands and consumers feel like they are working within the loyalty structure of only one brand.

The actual execution of how it is adopted and the customers' experience will depend on how benefits are accumulated for which activities (transactional or non-transactional). A typical closed-loop coffee shop rewards programme could result in the following customer experience: every time I buy a coffee I either get a percentage of my spend back in virtual cash in a digital wallet or accumulate points to be redeemed at a future time. Non-transactional activities – maybe the coffee brand wants me to refer a friend to the programme or update my contact details or share my morning barista experience on social media – could attract bonus points or cash back in a digital wallet. What differentiates closed-loop programmes from more complex multi-partner programmes is this: what the customer earns in rewards at a particular coffee shop are available for redemption only in the same coffee shop.

As mentioned in the previous chapter, a programme that does this well in South Africa is Vida e Caffè. All benefits are earned and redeemed within its rewards app, which also doubles up as a digital cash back wallet. Functionality like order ahead also exists within the wallet to enhance the coffee shop user experience. Other loyalty programmes may sometimes offer Vida coffee as a reward within their programme but this does not distract from Vida e Caffè's own programme, which remains simple and transparent in a closed-loop structure. Darren Levy, CEO of Vida e Caffè, connects the success of its programme's simplicity and the closed-loop structure: "We have always operated a closed-loop loyalty programme. In 2015 we migrated from a card to a mobile loyalty and payments app that enabled us to offer many exclusive benefits and more functionality."

> **With our loyalty benefits, programme simplicity, and ensuring earn and spend is retained within our store network, we drive customer loyalty and retention as well as attract new customers.**
> **— Darren Levy, CEO Vida e Caffè**

Chapter 22

Coalition Loyalty – Working together for customers and brands

Coalition programmes, where members collect and redeem at a long list of partner brands, make sense for both customers and partners. The model has been used around the world, with brands like Nectar, PayBack, Airmiles, Dotz, and FlyBuys becoming household names in the markets in which they operate. Why then are they not seen in all markets, and why is creating a successful coalition programme so hard? To help answer this, Iain Pringle, Managing Partner New World Loyalty, who has a career of experience in building, launching and (in one case) closing coalition programmes in the UK and South Africa, is perfectly placed to shed light on the opportunities and challenges of the coalition model.

❝ —— Contribution by Iain Pringle

Aggregating value across multiple partners makes sense. It makes sense for customers who love the opportunity to collect points faster. It makes sense for the programme operators attracted by the opportunity to build a cash and data rich asset that investors love. But, above all, it makes sense for the participating brands because customers who spend at more retailers within a programme go on to spend more at the home brand. This was best demonstrated by Qantas in 2011 who shared that members who linked their programme to Woolworths increased travel spend on Qantas by 17% generating 850,000 incremental flights. Not bad from a population of 22 million!

But creating a successful coalition programme is hard. In the words of Bryan Pearson (past Chairman of LoyaltyOne, the owner and operator of Airmiles in Canada), the key skill is in "making the elephants dance". By this he means convincing large brands to put egos aside and work together for mutual benefit.

Members increased travel spend by 17%, generating 850,000 incremental flights.
— Iain Pringle

In recent years, however, the coalition model has fared less well with the failure of Plenti in the USA in 2018 and the loss of several key names from coalition programmes around the world. Experience from Nectar in the UK and Aeroplan in Canada also suggests that, while the case for coalitions still make sense, they probably work best under the ownership of a single lead brand.

If the purpose of loyalty is to give customers the greatest benefit in the shortest possible time, then the coalition model must work. The case is particularly strong for market follower brands competing with a dominant player, as they have the most to gain from joining forces with others. For this to be successful, loyalty leaders need to remember why joining with others made sense in the first place. Only then will they truly measure the impact that a partnership programme offers and put into context the inevitable stresses which come from any long-term relationship.

So watch this space on coalition programmes. The traditional model is under pressure today as brands seek first party data solutions, but the playing field is open for the tech giants to create cross-border currencies. The question is – which one will move first?

Chapter 23

Loyalty partnerships

Like a tsunami hitting the loyalty industry, we see partnerships exploding everywhere, between some of the least likely brands, but also with brands which make complete sense from the outset. No wonder it sometimes feels like the industry is promiscuous.

We are used to simple and logical partnerships, for example in the travel industry, where airlines and car rental or hotel companies are in partnership to enhance the traveller's journey with augmented programme rewards. Now, we see more complex or less obvious partnerships like Starbucks and Delta Airlines, where travellers can earn SkyMiles on their morning cappuccino. The banking industry is also a complex playground for loyalty partnerships, often offering so much more than rewards on credit card spend.

> **Partnerships are a differentiator for loyalty programmes. It needs to be a triple win for Nedbank, the partner, and of course the customer. — Dharmesh Bhana, Executive: Loyalty & Rewards Nedbank[22]**

Commercially, there is no question that there is an uplift if properly executed. It is well documented that if the loyalty member spends double that of a non-loyalty customer, you are likely to see more engagement with programme partners.

To share invaluable knowledge on a powerful partnership approach, I turn to David Slavick, Co-Founder and Partner at Ascendent Loyalty, which has created its own unique process methodology for loyalty partnerships: Uniting Loyalty®.

“ —— Contribution by David Slavick

At a time when not moving forward is equivalent to falling behind, partnerships are proving to be the missing piece in many successful loyalty programme game plans. There are key reasons why partnerships at both the strategic and tactical level are gaining traction in the loyalty world.

This isn't at all surprising given that, when executed properly, loyalty partnerships offer tremendous measurable lift for both parties: i.e. conversion rate, visit frequency, average order value, units per transaction, customer satisfaction and customer engagement, referrals and customer acquisition, to name a few.

Some of the key criteria to examine in setting up a loyalty partnership are:

- Does the potential partner have properly identified customers on their database?
- Do they have a permission-based relationship partnership construct?
- Do they have a geography that matches up to my geography?
- Is their audience size significant enough to make it worthwhile to make the investment to create the partnership?
- If an e-commerce store - is the website experience attractive to your customers?
- Is the partner's loyalty programme/business model attractive to my customers?
- Is the partner's loyalty programme omnichannel?

The need to provide 'freshness' and 'new news' will forge ahead, while loyalty partnerships will continue to increase in popularity in response to this phenomenon.

—— ”

Chapter 24

Is a subscription-based programme loyalty?

One of the undeniable trends in loyalty is the subscription-based approach. The million dollar question, however, is whether a subscription-based programme can be defined as a loyalty programme? I don't really care too much about definitions. I prefer to focus on outcomes.

Year after year we hear impressive statistics from Amazon regarding its Prime model, which could be argued to be on a pedestal in terms of its successful subscription programme. According to Statista, Amazon Prime report a 94% retention rate for members after year one, of which 98% remain subscribed into year three. Any company, whether it has a subscription programme, a loyalty programme, membership, or just product holding, would dream of retention statistics like these.

Why do consumers commit to a monthly or annual subscription? According to Clarus Commerce (rebranded ebbo), the top three paid-for benefits are: 1. free shipping, 2. instant discounts, and 3. faster shipping. Overwhelmingly, when the same question was asked of Amazon customers about joining Prime, the number one reason was faster and free shipping. Faster and free shipping remains the main reason why Prime customers renew their membership.

However, there are many interesting versions of paid-for, subscription-based loyalty programmes beyond the infamous Amazon Prime model. Most notably are coffee or smoothie subscription models, car wash programmes, tyre renewal programmes, and other retail programmes (like grocery and fashion). In fact, there are endless other industries, but these are the most prevalent.

In the coffee and smoothie world, brands like Panera Bread in the USA have boasted results such as increasing monthly frequency from four to ten visits, and food sales growth by 70%.[23] In the UK, Pret A Manger launched Club Pret in 2020:

> **Pret's subscription service, Club Pret, is redeemed 1.25 million times a week – up 11% year-on-year. — The Guardian[24]**

Many retail brands mirror Amazon Prime with their benefits. Some less obvious benefits are available in programmes like Tesco's ClubCard Plus, where consumers can get 10% off two shops of their choice each month. I am sure shoppers plan their Tesco shop carefully. Fashion retailers are also offering subscription programmes to either deliver a wardrobe solution each month with a sale or return policy, or rent a new outfit for renewable fashion ideas.

Do subscription programmes really change behaviour? The answer is yes, if executed well. A study by McKinsey & Company in 2020 confirmed that this is the case. Sixty-two percent of consumers are more likely to spend more on the brand and 43% are more likely to buy weekly since joining the paid loyalty programme.

Chapter 25

Strategy to programme management and everything inbetween

Probably the most used infographic within our company is what we define as Truth's-8 step process for a loyalty programme launch. Equally applicable is Truth's 9-step process for a loyalty programme re-design. This process allows us to describe the separate steps required from loyalty strategy as defined in chapter 17, to designing a programme, which we cover in vast detail throughout this book, through to post programme management against KPIs. There are numerous critical steps inbetween which claim their separate chapters in *Blind Loyalty*. In my opinion, if all else fails, just follow this guideline to progress to a successful launch.

Illustrated below is the 9-step process for a loyalty programme re-design. The 8-step process is the same, minus the current programme evaluation (in step 2). Source: Truth Loyalty Consultancy.

1

STRATEGY DEVELOPMENT

Most importantly, define the strategic rationale for the loyalty programme. At all times, the design must respond to these strategic levers to ensure loyalty is a business strategy and not just a marketing tool.

2

PROGRAMME AUDIT

Evaluate the current programme against an approved set of audit checks. These are outlined in the next chapter in Truth's blueprint for loyalty programme success. It is a simple and yet powerful check list. This will highlight strengths and opportunities for the re-design.

3 PROGRAMME DESIGN

Programme design: many chapters of this book cover elements of programme design, i.e. the customer programme experience. What will customers receive, via what channel and in response to which activities? This is the one step where creative juices can flow readily. Commercial checks can overlay caution later.

4 CONCEPT TESTING AND CUSTOMER RESEARCH

I passionately believe that all design options should be stress-tested in customer research. This can be as simple as a quantitative survey to your customer database or as robust as independently recruited focus groups. Either way, time must be built in to modify step 3 (programme design) should the research suggest it.

5 MEMBER ENGAGEMENT

What happens in the 12 months post launch is a critical element of how the customer will experience your loyalty programme. This 12-month member engagement plan should be defined up front in step 5. We cover this in depth in chapter 29.

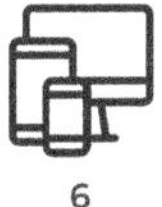

6 TECHNOLOGY PLATFORM

Technology will make or break the programme. Options will vary from in-house build to complete outsource to technical plug-ins, all jargon for a strategic technical plan to support, drive, and enhance the loyalty customer experience.

7 BUSINESS CASE / COMMERCIALS

Only after you have successfully defined your technical plan will you have enough input data to create a sound commercial case for the loyalty programme. Technology and other loyalty costs are only one side of the equation. Equally important is the commercial uplift from changed customer behaviour to prove the programme's ROI (see chapters 90-93).

8 PROJECT IMPLEMENTATION

Once the stakeholders have approved the loyalty business case, the real project work commences, with inter-dependencies driven against a critical path. This will have an impact on marketing, operations, HR/staff, IT, finance, legal, compliance, and other company departments. Loyalty is not in the silo of marketing alone.

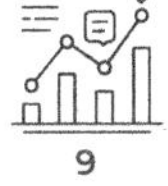

9 PROGRAMME MANAGEMENT AND KPIS

Post launch, we recommend daily, even hourly management of launch operations (even to the extent of creating a war room). Once the initial hype of launch is settled, the focus needs to be on company-wide loyalty KPIs and day-to-day programme management of the company's strongest customer asset.

Chapter 26

Blueprint for loyalty success: 10-point check list

There are 101 different ways to assess a loyalty programme's performance. The following ten points form part of a thorough audit check and can guide the operating brand on how best to improve its programme via quick wins or longer-term, strategic changes that may be required. Source: Truth Loyalty Consultancy.

Is the programme simple and easy for members to understand? Are the rules regarding earn, redemption, broader benefits, or tier changes transparent? i.e. Can the member easily access all programme rules and ultimately understand them?

Is the loyalty programme visible across all brand elements? This describes the opportunity to promote the loyalty programme in store, in branch, online, on social media, in partners' media space, and through all communications. Everything communicates!

We read in the previous chapter that member engagement is a critical part of designing a successful loyalty programme. Chapter 29 describes how to create a compelling member engagement structure for loyalty communications.

We must ensure that the loyalty programme does not add any friction to the customer experience with the brand. Too often this is unfortunately the case when members have to jump through hoops to enrol via an arduous process or receive benefits.

One of the most critical yet overlooked success factors of a loyalty programme is undoubtedy how much the staff love and understand the programme. We have countless examples of how this makes or breaks a programme's success. See chapter 40.

A loyalty programme needs to support its mother brand. We must never feel that it is at a juxtaposition to the operating brand. Fortunately, we mostly observe that this is not the case. Potential problems arise from partner selection in the programme. Brands must challenge themselves on brand fit, customer benefit, and commercial return when selecting programme partners.

The loyalty programme needs to offer benefits and worthwhile rewards to its members. Is it worth the effort of enrolment? Is it worth the effort of activities required to trigger rewards or tier changes? In particular, this audit check point needs to be evaluated against the competitive environment because consumers will most certainly be comparing programme reward levels.

Innovation for innovation's sake is meaningless but for a programme to remain relevant and offer newness, it needs to innovate as it evolves over time. Innovation doesn't need to refer to technical innovations but newness is often likely to be executed by new technological advancements. This either makes the experience more seamless or introduces fun via gamification and the like.

Without question, the operating brand should be receiving data on how members engage, activity levels, and programme performance. Broader customer data may also be gathered (for example on transaction spend/behaviour). Strategic extraction of data insight is a critical part of a loyalty programme's success.

There are many critical numerical performance indicators for loyalty programmes. We discuss these in detail in chapter 94. Programme operators need to be able to measure key metrics like incremental sales performance, activity rates, and percentage of sales through the loyalty programme, to name a few.

Chapter 27

Simple and transparent

You may think that this chapter title doesn't seem significant enough to merit so much focus. I would strongly argue otherwise. I believe we have experienced a revolution – not evolution – in terms of how programmes have simplified over the recent half decade. Thank goodness for the sanity of our loyal customers.

Let's take the South African banking and insurance industry, the home of many award-winning loyalty brands. Five or ten years ago, I'd have been highly critical of the unnecessary complexity of the programmes. It was virtually impossible to truly work out exactly how you could extract maximum value. This loyalty sector certainly left members with a sense of distrust for the operating brand because the programmes seemed deliberately impossible to understand. They were neither simple nor transparent. However, we need to be cognisant that to deliver a profitable and yet innovative customer-focused loyalty proposition requires some element of complexity to commercially safeguard the operating loyalty brand. Tiering is probably the most commonly used loyalty function to enable big headline reward levels for the most engaged customers and marketing straplines.

We are not against the use of tiering. For the right industry and right brand, I fully support the benefits for both customers and for the loyalty brand. In particular, where bank-wide loyalty programmes are rewarding for more than just the credit card swipe, tiering enables the banks to position top earners within top tiers. This enables the most loyal customers to gain maximum rewards because they have engaged across maximum products, touchpoints, and desired banking behaviours.

> **The brands that just focus on card swipes will receive nothing more than tennis elbow!**
> **— James Rheeder, ex Absa Rewards**

I truly believe that loyalty brands have leap-frogged forward into the age of making life easier for their members to understand and not have to jump over a thousand hurdles to earn a free coffee. Whilst some complexities, like tiering, may still need to exist, they do so with more transparency. The winners allow customers to see how they can earn more if they are not maximising their loyalty potential. There is no need for a nuclear science degree to enjoy your loyalty bounty any more because the best programmes explain how you can enjoy greater rewards and these are proactively communicated to you.

Earlier in this chapter we refer to the South African banking industry. One of the standout loyalty winners in this industry is FNB eBucks. eBucks messages me monthly with a call to action to complete a particular banking behaviour to reap better rewards. Once I log into the app or website pages, a cute orange minion figure guides me through a ladder of improvements so that next month I can earn more. Obviously, the bank also reaps its return if I move up the ladder and improve my tiering because to do so I will have become a better banking client through ticking off desired behaviours (which includes taking out more banking products). This is a prime example of transparency even if there is still room to improve on simplicity.

Chapter 28

Visibility: don't hide. Loyalty is worth shouting about!

Typically, much expenditure is invested in a loyalty programme launch and ongoing management. Sadly, many brands make the mistake of almost treating the loyalty programme as a temporary campaign after launch and the visibility of the programme disappears. This is a catastrophic mistake. The loyalty programme needs to be an 'always-on' strategy and proposition for members to see and be reminded about at every touch point.

Think about your preferred loyalty retail brand: first, imagine the store environment. The most used loyalty programmes do not leave their customers to guess if there is a loyalty programme or not. It is front and centre across the store and all communication channels.

> **There is a direct correlation between programme success and visibility of the loyalty experience across all touchpoints.**

In the store, there will be loyalty offers available throughout. There will be clear point of sale material for programme sign up and programme awareness. The online ecommerce store should also drive programme awareness, usage, and acquisition throughout the various online customer journeys.

We need to consider the communication environment throughout the loyalty ecosystem. Over the years, we have started to see the good, the bad, and the ugly in terms of programme visibility. It breaks my loyalty heart to receive brand emailers promoting product and offers with zero mention of the loyalty programme that the brand and products belong to. This, unfortunately, still occurs often from brands not yet fully committed to the power of loyalty and customer centricity.

Social media posts, web presence, and brand communications across all channels need to sing from the same loyalty song sheet. It is the biggest missed opportunity when brands don't fully integrate loyalty into their full marketing mix.

If we look at more traditional media, brands have moved from previously using a postage stamp-sized icon at the bottom of above-the-line communications to whole billboards screaming the praises of its loyalty accolades. Naturally, we prefer the latter.

Don't forget the importance of visibility of your loyalty brand in the programme partners' loyalty assets. Imagine a fuel company which is part of a banking loyalty programme. There should be no confusion to the customer when they fill up their vehicle. Can I or can I not receive loyalty benefits? How visible is the brand presence of the partners across the fuel forecourt in the fuel partnership example? Partnership programmes often fall short of loyalty brand promotion and end up missing the mark in terms of loyalty programme visibility.

Chapter 29

Member engagement: success factor number one

Too much focus is placed on the loyalty programme launch and too little real planning goes into ongoing loyalty programme engagement post launch. We insist that the first 12 months of the member experience needs to be planned, mapped out, and designed into the member communications and into the loyalty technical build and capability.

For simplicity, we split the various elements of member engagement into four pillars. It is possible to plan and manage them as independent pillars but optimal loyalty programme management and integrated communications require the four pillars to co-exist and work together.

Member engagement communication framework

Each pillar will be fully explained in the next few chapters. In my opinion, member engagement justifies a whole loyalty book of its own.

If we start with the **acquisition** pillar, loyalty acquisition plans differ from traditional above-the-line media. Your marketing agency may need assistance in how to make this differentiation, otherwise hard-earned media costs may be wasted. See chapter 31 for the breakdown of how to plan for the loyalty launch and member acquisition.

The second pillar is the foundation of a solid loyalty engagement plan. Without fail, make sure the **loyalty operational communications** are seamlessly planned and executed. This is the backbone of your member engagement strategy. Unpack this further in chapter 32.

All marketers will know how to deliver the promotional pillar of the member engagement plan (see chapter 33). Some refer to it as the retail calendar, others simply call it the **marketing calendar**. It is a month-by-month annualised promotional communications plan that never misses a beat for the festive season, Mother's Day, Easter, Valentine's Day, and the like. The critical approach here, is to use content from this 'always-on' communications plan within the loyalty operations delivery to avoid a string of disparate and repetitive communications.

Finally, pillar four creates the essence of personalisation and relevance through a **lifestyle communications** approach. This is only possible once customer segments are established with strategic objectives, which the member engagement plan can drive. Chapter 34 dives deeper into this pillar.

In terms of style of communication, the use of educational marketing can prove so much more powerful than traditional media, including podcasts and informative loyalty content.

Chapter 30

Personalisation – most used word in the industry for a reason

In the final section of the *2022 Truth and BrandMapp South African Loyalty Whitepaper*, I debate the power of personalisation.

❝ —— Contribution by Truth and BrandMapp Loyalty Whitepaper

If ever there was a buzzword around CRM and loyalty, it is 'personalisation'. We hear retailers sending us 'personalised' vouchers, we hear loyalty managers talking about personalisation as their number one priority, but at the end of the day, does it matter to the members of loyalty programmes? The annual customer research from BrandMapp shows clearly that loyalty brands which were ranked highly for offering personalised and relevant rewards, were ranked equally highly in 'the loyalty brand I cant live without!' The research results show a direct correlation between the two measures: i.e. personalisation and relevance matters to consumers.

Personalisation is essential in building customer loyalty. For communications to be effective, they need to be relevant. Absence of personalisation leads to valueless noise; without personalisation, customers become dis-engaged and leave your brand. We recommend that loyalty programmes must stay relevant on two levels – firstly, in terms of their rewards offered; and secondly, in terms of relevant communications. Customers don't respond purely to loyalty programme incentives, but rather to the brand's relevance to their own individual needs.

—————— ❞

> **Personalisation is becoming a way of life for many brands. Collecting personal profile information on your customers, crafting personalised experiences around them, and creating solid long-term relationships that foster brand loyalty. — Clarus Commerce[25]**

The quote above, from Clarus Commerce (rebranded ebbo), refers to collecting personal information, which obviously must be done within the forever changing and improving legislation surrounding personal data collection and usage. Layering the personal profile data with behavioural data and other external data enrichment gives brands the ability to create such sophistication in profiling that we could finally be reaching the segment of one (customer).

Fionna Ronnie, Head of Customer & Loyalty at The Foschini Group (TFG), describes the retailer's ability to create personalised loyalty experiences from billions and billions of data points. The TFG Rewards programme is hinged on its ability to offer personalised rewards.

I believe grocery retailers excel in personalisation due to the sheer volume of data points they have to play with. Mix this with lashings of AI on a base of solid data and voilà - personalisation. The Danish retailer Salling launched its entire loyalty programme, now with 11 million members, based on personalised offers and loyalty experiences. There are no points or base earn rates. Its technology provider, Cheetah Digital (rebranded Marigold), claims Salling enjoys ten times more activity using personalised offers through its programme.

To summarise this chapter, refer back to chapter 5, where personalisation is a critical element within the 10Ps of loyalty marketing to supplement Kotler's 4Ps and the 7Ps of service marketing. Personalisation, Programme and Philosophy comprise the final 3Ps of Truth's loyalty marketing.

Chapter 31

Customer acquisition

If I had a bitcoin for every time I saw a misspent marketing dollar being ploughed into customer acquisition rather than customer retention, I would be deeply enjoying cryptocurrency trading. On a more serious note, loyalty programmes are not usually a mechanism for pure customer acquisition. They can be a powerful acquisition tool but we should rather focus on retention and customer value than pure acquisition in our loyalty efforts.

There are two standout examples where I wish the relevant organisations really thought more about their long-term loyal customers. Firstly, we all know the old promotional campaign that invites us to 'take out our retail store card and we will give you $100 in shopping vouchers'. At first glance, this may look competitive or enticing, but the negative impact on the loyal store card customer cannot be underestimated. The loyal customer of 20 years has used the financial product or shopped at the store, duly paying her bill, on time, each month. This has nothing to do with a loyalty programme and everything to do with customer loyalty.

Secondly, sports and fitness clubs are famously fighting a battle against customer attrition. It is often stated that annually at least half a fitness club membership base leaves the club. It is therefore essential to refill the leaky bucket of club members. I can't criticise acquisition campaigns that entice new members with a free first month or sports kit upon sign up. These all seem like perfectly appropriate enrolment incentives. However, the loyal club member who has been a member for many years and pays their monthly fees on time may feel unloved and unappreciated. This is a classic call-to-action to offer the acquisition incentive while simultaneously honouring the long-standing loyal customer and ensuring they feel appreciated. Obviously, this is where a loyalty programme can play its role to offer incentives on engagement and tenure. Virgin Active is featured in chapter 98.

I like to refer to a model created by REAP Consulting:

The power of retention and penetration — REAP

The real positive impact is yielded through 'R' for retention and 'P' for penetration. Chapter 98 discusses retention further. Penetration refers to the penetration of the customer's wallet: can the brand incentivise the customer to spend more or hold more of its products? The 'E' in REAP stands for efficiencies - cost and operational efficiencies. The 'A' is for acquisition. Neither 'E' or 'A' will stack up as the key drivers for a positive business case for a new loyalty initiative without a strong input from 'R' and 'P'.

When a new programme is launched, we often see acquisition statistics achieve the following targets. If there is a strong marketing campaign to drive acquisition of new members and migration of existing members, 35% of customers targeted to sign up in the first year should be possible in the first month. Month two should see a further 15% of the full year target enrol and thereafter a run rate of approximately 5% per month should aid your calculations of monthly acquisition. These are the approximate acquisition numbers we use for business case calculations.

Chapter 32

Loyalty operational communications

Without question, loyalty operational communications is the key engagement pillar of a loyalty programme. In a nutshell, this section outlines what communications a programme operator must send to its carefully acquired membership base. Without such a plan, loyalty members will feel lost, unloved, and unappreciated in the loyalty experience they signed up for. Even if they are earning handsome rewards, if the brand isn't promptly and impactfully communicating such rewards and experiences, the member will feel short-changed. At Truth, we propose the structure below as the basis of the loyalty operational communications plan.

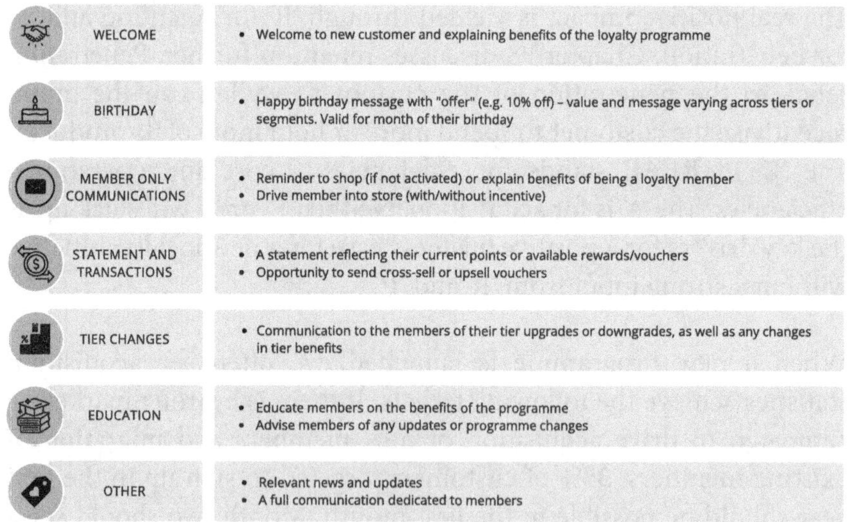

WELCOME	• Welcome to new customer and explaining benefits of the loyalty programme
BIRTHDAY	• Happy birthday message with "offer" (e.g. 10% off) – value and message varying across tiers or segments. Valid for month of their birthday
MEMBER ONLY COMMUNICATIONS	• Reminder to shop (if not activated) or explain benefits of being a loyalty member • Drive member into store (with/without incentive)
STATEMENT AND TRANSACTIONS	• A statement reflecting their current points or available rewards/vouchers • Opportunity to send cross-sell or upsell vouchers
TIER CHANGES	• Communication to the members of their tier upgrades or downgrades, as well as any changes in tier benefits
EDUCATION	• Educate members on the benefits of the programme • Advise members of any updates or programme changes
OTHER	• Relevant news and updates • A full communication dedicated to members

Loyalty operational communication framework

Upon enrolment, members must receive a **welcome** message. According to Antavo (an enterprise loyalty solution), 74% of new programme subscribers expect a welcome email and open rates are typically at 50%, 86% higher than average email open rates. Antavo's research shows that subscribers who receive the welcome email show a 33% longer term engagement with the loyalty brand.

A simple **birthday** message can go a long way, but loyalty brands shouldn't waste marketing costs on just sending a message (this can be reserved for family and friends!). Birthday loyalty communications should be accompanied with a birthday gift (e.g. double points or 10% off your next store visit).

Member-only communications are often what brands automatically send out to the loyalty database, alerting members about member-only benefits like pre-sale early released prices for members.

Statement & transactions must be available to members at every touch point (website or app) and after each transaction (earn or redeem). A monthly statement of transactions and tier status is recommended and there is nothing more powerful than receiving an alert to confirm the value you've just received from a loyalty brand. However, sometimes there may be a reverse psychological effect, which we outline in chapter 99.

Tier changes are a particularly emotive part of the loyalty experience – positive and negative. If these are handled well, with informative communications alerting a potential tier downgrade, members can try to rescue the imminent tier change by changing their next flight, store transaction, or credit card swipe. Airline frequent flyer programmes have been managing these sensitive scenarios for decades.

Last but not least, **educational** content about the loyalty programme is critical. Members need to be updated, informed, and reminded of how the programme works, especially if there are changes to programme rules and new benefits.

Chapter 33

Annual marketing calendar

To help the loyalty communications come alive, close integration with the annual marketing calendar is critical. They are not separate communications plans and there are certainly not different customers on the receiving end. We must always remember that the same customer receives multiple communications from the brand, either for loyalty, brand promotional activities, or other operational communications.

> **Fully engaged customers deliver 23% premium over the average customer in share of wallet, profitability, and revenue. — Capgemini[26]**

So what is the marketing calendar? Simply put, the marketing calendar is how a brand communicates its offering in relation to calendarised events like Mother's/Father's Day, Valentine's Day, religious celebrations, school holidays, and well-known promotional periods like Black Friday and the festive season (regardless of religion).

The loyalty programme should play a powerful role in how a brand communicates campaigns and offers during the various marketing calendar promotional periods. For example, "*You get double points on Mother's Day gifting and treats.*" In the banking environment,

"Let us help you save after the festive season with a higher savings interest rate for loyalty members on any deposits made in January." These simple communications and integrated offers bring relevance and impact from the loyalty programme over and above what the brand can offer without the programme.

A classic annual marketing calendar may look something like this example below:

Framework for annual marketing calendar

This chapter doesn't attempt to unpack the channel preferences for loyalty and marketing communications. We realise that this is a rapidly changing landscape and there are experts in the marketing industry who understand media and channel choice much more profoundly than we do. When we work with clients on their loyalty member engagement plan, we happily hand over the required work on creative execution and channel or media buying to the agency networks that exist to deliver both professionally.

Chapter 34

Lifestyle segmented communications

The overriding theme of every chapter in this book screams personalisation from the loyalty roof tops. Our final pillar of the member engagement plan cements this theory firmly into the strategic approach to delivering loyalty communications.

The illustration below showcases something extremely obvious. However, despite the customer-centric approach obviously being better for longer term success, it is so often sacrificed for the execution of a campaign-centric approach.

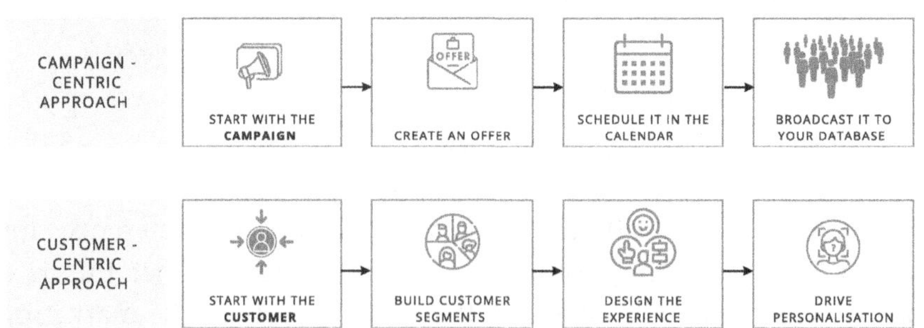

Campaign-centric versus customer-centric approach

Why is this the case? In the simplest terms, most organisations are product centric rather than customer centric. Therefore, campaigns that drive product objectives (like new product launches or sales volumes) do not start with the customer in mind, but rather with the unit sales target per product or service on offer. The risk with a campaign-centric approach is the execution via 'broadcast to your database'. The carefully acquired database is not an available target audience for spam mail to drive last minute sales initiatives. This is the most harmful way to treat your permission-based database.

In a customer-centric environment, segments are created from strategic data input. Utopia is a segment of one but this is rarely executed at scale. We can refer back to the early years of grocery retail, when Tesco pioneered the power of data with its partner Dunnhumby via Tesco ClubCard. Rumour has it that within the quarterly vouchers distributed to 16 million plus members with at least four different offers, no more than four mailers were ever the same. The magical power of data and personalisation, which today isn't seen as pioneering, is essential to keep your communications relevant to loyalty members.

> **Emirates Skywards emails have 86 variants based on tiering, number of miles, and engagement with partners. This doubles the email open rate at a minimum.**
> **— Dr Nejib Ben-Khedher, Head of Emirates Skywards[27]**

Strategic lifestyle segments are easy to establish if data is collected, managed, and analysed. Execution of a segmented lifestyle plan is more challenging if the organisation isn't customer centric. The business needs to understand why this is the best approach not only for loyalty but for the entire organisation. This loops full circle back to customer centricity, which we introduced in chapter 8.

Chapter 35

Predict your way to a higher ROI

The term predictive modelling has many interpretations but, if executed excellently, it can yield almost unmatchable results. This requires predictive analytical input into campaign planning, data extraction, actual analysis, and not forgetting creative execution itself.

What is predictive modelling? In campaigns and communications, as the name suggests, it is a methodology that predicts how a consumer will behave in response to the offer or incentive designed for them. Unfortunately, the majority of campaign planning time is given to the look and feel of the creative execution instead of the strategy and delivery of accurate data or offer selection.

For purpose of illustration, let's take a luxury product like lingerie from a retailer selling high-end clothing, beauty, luxury luggage, and homeware products in London. From analysis, the customer who currently buys lingerie from such a store is also displaying the following transactional characteristics:

1. The customers fall within the top tier of the value segmentation.
2. They never buy homewear products from this retailer.
3. They frequently buy cosmetics from various beauty houses at the store.
4. They shop at least once per quarter.
5. They buy heavily from promotional campaigns.

None of these transactional indicators are directly attributed to the lingerie category; this is deliberate. If the identified five indicators are applied in the data selection for the next lingerie campaign, the targeted audience may well be smaller than a 'spray-and-pray' approach but I guarantee the campaign will achieve more positive response rates (almost regardless of the creative execution or, possibly, even the offer itself).

It is reassuring to know that such basic predictive modelling techniques have advanced and the example above is overly simplified to best illustrate the principles of predictive modelling. Not only can advanced analytics assist the commercial minded CRM and loyalty organisations, but we also see how often the application of such modelling can help a higher purpose, too.

Retail purchases of pain and indigestion medication (up to eight months before diagnosis) have been found to be strong predictive indicators of ovarian cancer.

> **Shop loyalty card data may help spot ovarian cancer.**
> **— Michelle Roberts, BBC[28]**

In chapter 14, I share the insights from an interview I had with Dr Shorful Islam. In this interview, he discloses how he has had the privilege of working with charitable organisations to empower greater donations and higher success rates for fund raising using similar data techniques used in commercial predictive modeling.

Chapter 36

Customer lifecycle

Customer relationships are not linear. Customer lifecycle management differs from customer lifestyle segmentation (chapter 34) in that it is not based on customer preferences or value, but rather on how a customer is progressing through their relationship with the brand. Often lifecycle management is more easily applied (and understood) in financial services products. Banks are particularly strong at managing the lifecycle of their clients from onboarding through to engagement to maximise customer lifetime value (CLTV).

We have simplified the lifecycle stages as below:-

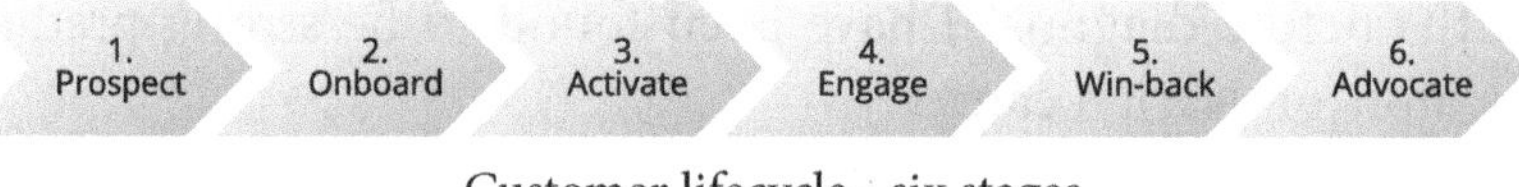

Customer lifecycle - six stages

Loyalty programmes clearly play a role in the various phases of a customer's lifecycle. As I suggested in chapter 31, customer acquisition (i.e. **prospecting** in stage 1) may not be the most impactful loyalty lever to pull. Once a customer has joined the brand, as we outlined earlier in our member engagement chapters, a welcome communication to **onboard** your customer is critical (stage 2). Customers expect this; they need it.

Stage 3, the **activation** stage, goes one step further than welcoming new members to your loyalty programme or brand. Your data analysis will show you that the onboarding process hasn't worked hard enough and targeted customers need further enticement to start engaging with the programme or to transact with the brand. This may take the form of incentives (discount or booster points).

Once activated, customers tend to **engage** more easily with the brand and programme (stage 4). Previous chapters on member engagement highlight the importance of continuous relationship marketing, and this cannot be stressed strongly enough.

Inevitably, customers will start to fall away. Retention is key but attrition will find its harmful way into your database. At different stages of a customer's relationship, there are more dangerous attrition points. For example, when a mobile phone contract is due for renewal, or at the end of the calendar year to re-new a medical aid or insurance plan. Knowing this allows programme operators to mitigate these risks and increase renewal. If the customer has already left your brand, **win-back** strategies are required (stage 5).

Finally (in stage 6), should customers renew or continue their relationship with the brand (i.e. skip stage 5), true brand **advocacy** can be experienced where customers become the most powerful sales and marketing tool.

> **From the first spark of interest in your product to the very last purchase they make with your brand, lifecycle marketing focuses on identifying the best ways to engage each customer based on where they are in the customer lifecycle.**
> **— RESCI[29]**

Chapter 37

Loyalty communications: not the same old same old!

I am not a copywriter or creative director. Such skill sets sit way out of my sphere of talent and I always seek the assistance of experienced and capable CRM agencies to fulfil these roles. This is the only chapter that possibly touches on the more creative agency work critical to successful loyalty communications. It requires a different skill set to write for a CRM plan versus a traditional ATL (above-the-line) marketing plan.

How is it different? Put simply, loyalty communications have a role to play in educating newly acquired or long-standing members on how to maximise the programme. The more a member engages with the loyalty programme, the longer they will stay with the brand. Therefore, customer lifetime value increases and the loyalty programme becomes more successful in reaching KPIs. On the other hand, most ATL communications are tasked with attracting, acquiring, and enticing customers to transact with your brand.

How is this achieved? We believe passionately in a few principles that guide loyalty communications.

Firstly, we encourage the use of iconography to help members navigate their way through the loyalty journey. The iconography can offer step-by-step guidance on programme rules and how to earn and redeem benefits.

Secondly, the language must be simple and impactful. The copywriter needs to say more with fewer words. Loyalty programmes can be complicated (but hopefully not – please see chapter 27), so simple language is required. This can often be vastly different to traditional agency copywriting which aims to be creative, intelligent, or witty. There is, of course, a place for this here if it can aid the member's absorption of key facts about the programme. Often the language is more 'dry', factual, and less wordy, which should result in more impactful loyalty communications.

Thirdly, as is the recurring theme throughout this book, there must be as much personalisation as possible, depending on how much data has been acquired at that stage of the customer journey. Obviously, for a welcome email, very little is known about the member so personalisation may be limited as data insight is limited.

Finally, there needs to be a consistent loyalty lexicon for the loyalty programme. This is explained in detail in the next chapter, but in a nutshell, answer the following question: 'Is a point a point or a perk or a coin?' Loyalty programmes have a language of their own to match the loyalty brand and we call this the loyalty lexicon.

For illustration purposes, here is an extract of the welcome email from Sephora's Beauty Insider programme showcasing simple, yet impactful language and a step-by-step process (with numerical iconography) on how to maximise your membership in the programme.

Sephora Beauty Insider - Welcome email

Chapter 38

What on earth is a loyalty lexicon?

I'm not someone who enjoys marketing jargon. I try to simplify the crazy language of loyalty and the unnecessary complexity of loyalty programmes. In order to achieve this in the loyalty communications plan, the programme manager must establish what we refer to as a 'loyalty lexicon'. Given the reaction of most loyalty professionals we work with, I realise that this may sound like jargon. It is, however, critical that all your brand points sing clearly from the same loyalty song sheet when communicating the programme.

When we pull together loyalty communications and critical support features like FAQs (frequently asked questions) and Ts&Cs (terms & conditions), all loyalty features, including the earn currency, must resonate in the same loyalty brand language.

> **The loyalty lexicon is the foundation of the loyalty brand. Everything cascades from this structure to simplify your customers' understanding of your loyalty programme.**

We had the privilege of working with an incredible brand in Mauritius called IBL, which launched wiiv Rewards. This is a great example of a loyalty lexicon.

wiiv members are called 'wiivers'. They 'earn' points and, when they wish to redeem points, they 'spend' points. When wiivers get discounts in store from member-only pricing, they 'save money'.

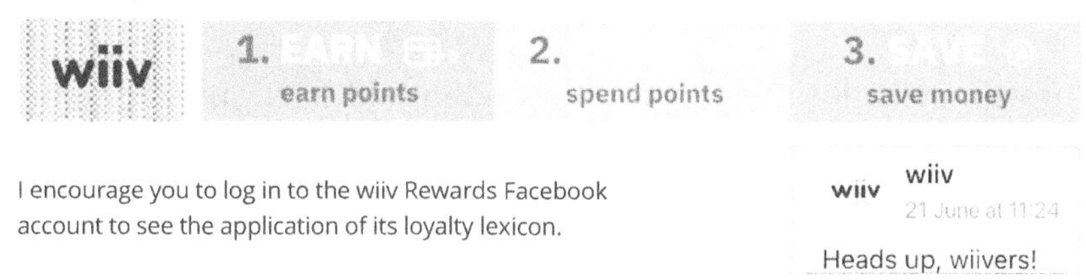

wiiv Rewards as an example of a loyalty lexicon

The list of elements to be included in the lexicon should include, but most certainly not be limited to (our example illustrated here is Pick n Pay's Smart Shopper programme):-

* Loyalty strap line: e.g. 'It's our way of saying thank you.'
* Term for members: e.g. 'Smart Shoppers'
* Currency: e.g. 'Smart Points'
* Verb to join: e.g. 'Join'
* Verb to collect rewards: e.g. 'Earn'
* Verb to redeem: e.g. 'Switch'

Chapter 39

Seamless experience

This chapter epitomises how the customer should experience every brand element, not just the loyalty programme. Naturally, in this book we are focused on the loyalty programme experience, but a seamless brand experience can engender deeper customer loyalty than any points and prizes.

Unfortunately, loyalty programmes often add friction to the brand experience. They require one extra step to register, or one extra click for the customer to confirm their acceptance of the programme's Ts&Cs or privacy policy. Just one extra click can turn potential members off from joining your programme or earning rewards. I always encourage the sign up process to be as simple and quick as possible. Leave the interesting questions about hobbies and interests to a later stage in the member relationship. Programme operators can use loyalty points and incentives to persuade members to give future data points and insights about themselves.

We have recently seen a number of grocery retailers launch their loyalty programmes with single-minded launch campaigns: 'Open your loyalty account in less than two minutes (in any channel of your choice!)'. Is it the two minutes that will encourage me to engage or the channel of choice? I think it's the two-minute promise that draws me in and then I am additionally impressed that I can choose to register through WhatsApp, app, website, USSD, or at the till point. Ask for the minimum amount of required information to ensure a member is quickly registered. Worry about data enrichment later once the newly acquired member trusts you.

> **Good customer experience drives customer loyalty. Companies that deliver a better customer experience tend to retain more of their customers, get more incremental purchases from their customers, and attract more new customers through positive word of mouth. — Forrester[30]**

This all sounds so obvious but making it happen requires a slick loyalty ecosystem with a single view of the customer across all channels. This is the only way you can create a unified brand experience, which includes the various loyalty touchpoints. A unified experience can build trust which, ultimately, is the cornerstone of the customer relationship playground.

At the risk of belabouring the point, personalisation is key. If the loyalty programme offers a personalised and on point experience, customers feel special and understood, which helps build trust.

Finally, the seamless experience mandate can be enhanced or broken if things go wrong. All brands can unfortunately under-deliver or break a brand promise. How the problem is resolved can determine the future level of trust and brand love from the customer, which will determine a customer's determination to engage in or disengage from its loyalty programme.

Chapter 40

Loved by your people

Without question, the starting point for a successful loyalty programme is with your own people. It is clear to customers when staff have not been trained, motivated, and engaged within the company's loyalty offering.

I recently had the pleasure of interviewing Lindsay Eichten from TGI Fridays regarding the launch of Fridays Rewards in May 2023. The formulation of Fridays Rewards started with frontline staff and understanding where the company needed to improve the programme. Once the frontline team were excited and engaged with the Fridays Rewards programme, it became a much more powerful brand asset.

> **"The new Fridays Rewards was launched after meticulously examining moments that have led to guest or server teams' dissatisfaction, scrutinising them with a fine-tuned microscope. — Lindsay Eichten, Director CRM, Loyalty, & Media TGI Fridays[31]**

I believe that most loyalty programmes could improve staff engagement in the loyalty programme simply by launching a parallel employee loyalty initiative. There are often restrictions to such an idea if employees also receive discounts as an employment perk but for staff to love and promote a loyalty programme, they need to understand it deeply. There is no better way to achieve this than a parallel programme. To offer further insight on how strategically important staff engagement is, Pavel Los shares his thoughts from over 20 years at Shell, where he managed the global loyalty portfolio.

“ —— Contribution by Pavel Los

Frontline staff are the face of any business and their impact on customer loyalty cannot be underestimated. They are the ones who interact with customers on a daily basis and, as a result, they play a crucial role in the success of any loyalty programme.

> “ **Happy staff = happy customers = happy shareholders.**
> **— Pavel Los**

As a loyalty manager, it’s essential to engage your frontline staff properly. Educate them, train them, and explain the why and objectives of the loyalty programme. Without their buy-in, the execution of the programme is bound to fail. Customers can tell when frontline staff are not engaged with a loyalty programme and this can affect their perception of the entire business. The execution of a loyalty programme is critical because execution is the only strategy that customers see. If the execution is poor, customers will be dissatisfied and leave.

Happy staff equals happy customers, which equals happy shareholders. Engaged frontline staff understand how the loyalty programme benefits the customers and the business. This happiness can translate into better customer service, which can ultimately result in more loyal customers and higher spend from loyal customers.

I can’t overstate the importance of frontline staff fully supporting a loyalty programme.

—————— ”

Chapter 41

Matches brand values

This chapter is dedicated to reiterating that the loyalty programme should never veer off course in terms of its branding versus the mother brand. I am no branding expert but I certainly 'feel' it when a loyalty programme is not comfortable in its mother brand's skin.

Most of the time this is not an issue and consumers never give it a second thought. Unless there is strategically a different purpose for the loyalty programme, it exists only to advance business performance, customer satisfaction, and customer lifetime value. Therefore, it must be aligned to the mother brand.

> **The loyalty programme is a subset of its mother brand. All elements of the loyalty programme must resonate with the customer against the same brand values.**

We see this successfully play out in the following brand example. Discovery Vitality's programme is featured in chapter 79. The Vitality programme rewards members for living healthy lives (in personal health and financial wellness). Discovery is a healthcare provider, a bank, and an insurer. It therefore makes sense that its loyalty programme, Vitality, fully supports this in its rewards structure for transactional and non-transactional behaviours (health and banking). Vitality also operates with a partnership network and the partners, which are truly aligned to its mother brand's (Discovery) brand values, fall within its HealthyDining, HeathyFood, and HealthyCare network. If Vitality brought in a liquor store or fast food burger restaurant as a partner, the partnership would be 'off brand'. Obviously, it never has and never would, as the partnership would be opposed to the mother brand values.

We often experience a loyalty programme adding positively to the company's brand values, which is first prize. Take, for example, a running shoe store that rewards its members for all things running. This is entirely 'on brand'.

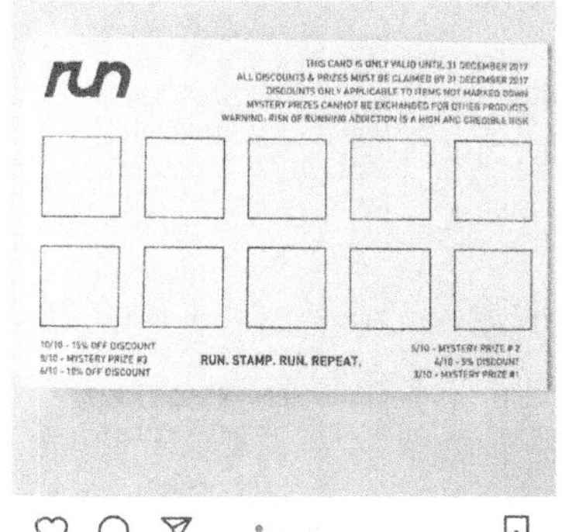

141 likes

run_storeza Ever think about running and wonder "I wish someone would just give me cool stuff when I run"? You are in luck! As of this week Wednesday (11 Oct) we will be starting our weekly runs at both stores.
Here is the fun part. When you join one of our runs, you get this cool card. And every time you run, we stamp it for you. The more stamps you accumulate, the more cool stuff you get.

We see this appealing stamp card at a store called 'run', which specialises in running shoes. It operates a simple stamp card. Each time the customer meets at the store for a group run, a stamp gets added. As their Instagram post states, 'the more you run, the more stamps you accumulate and the more cool stuff you get!' I love this! This completely matches its brand values.

'run' stamp card

Chapter 42

6 Building blocks to a loyalty programme design

The loyalty programme design is the starting point for any loyalty programme launch. I like to simplify it down to six initial blocks or questions. These questions, however, can only be addressed after the company has defined its loyalty strategy. Earlier chapters in the book drive the right approach to creating a loyalty strategy and with this in mind, the design can be created to ensure the strategy is adhered to and effectively upheld.

The six building blocks are:

Building blocks to the loyalty design. Source: Truth Loyalty Consultancy

1. What is the programme framework? See chapter 20, which outlines the different structures a programme can take. Is it a closed-loop programme, a coalition, a player or partner programme, or a subscription-based offering?

2. Who will join the loyalty programme? Is it a B2C (business to consumer), B2B (business to business), B2B2B (business to business to business), or a B2E (business to employee) programme? Will all consumers get the same programme or is there a segmented approach to the overt offering (we expect a segmented approach for the covert programme)?

3. Which behaviours will the programme reward? This must refer back to the programme strategy. Why is the company creating a loyalty programme? The programme must address this through what behaviours it expects its members to change and be rewarded for. We unpack this further in the next two chapters.

4. What benefits will the programme offer? Loyalty executives' creative juices can go wild with question four. There is a limitless inventory of benefits; therein lies the challenge. The value proposition for the members must be relevant and personalised. So, whilst there are so many options, the loyalty team must make sure they are appropriate to reward the behaviours in question three and motivate the right customers.

5. The programme rules will depend on the design from steps one to four. Typically, in this building block, we aim to address issues around expiry of points, tier rules or tiering at all, and auto enrolment upon product uptake (for example in financial services). We offer more insight into these rules in chapters 56-59.

6. Through which channels and touchpoints will the programme engage with members? Will the programme be digital only or have a card? Will there be a member portal and, if so, with what functionality? This is a very important building block to ensure that the experience is frictionless and aligned to your customer segment.

Chapter 43

Behaviours to reward: transactional

Traditionally, loyalty programmes rewarded for transactional behaviour only. Spend $10 and get a green shield stamp. Spend $100 and earn 1% cash value back in points. Fly on ten airline sectors and get miles and progress towards your tier upgrade.

So many programmes only reward transactional behaviour but the more engaging programmes incentivise both transactional and non-transactional behaviours. We introduce the depth and breadth of non-transactional behaviours in the next chapter.

> **Transactional behavioural rewards still remain the cornerstone of most loyalty programmes.**

It is worth comparing the various transactional loyalty options that can be used across different industries to achieve different objectives. Let's begin with retail. Transactional behaviours can include total basket spend in store, online, or on an app, or the combination of omnichannel purchases. Retailers often state that the omnichannel customer spends more than the single channel customer. Rewarding for category specific or SKU level is common, either by points allocation or discounts at point of sale. A common loyalty promotion is '3 for 2' offers exclusively for loyalty members. Rewarding on frequency has become a powerful driver of transactional behaviour change. The German retailer, Kik, through the MyKIK programme, rewards its members on frequency by offering a 20% discount off one item of the member's choice after five visits to the store. We often see restaurants – sit down or quick service (QSR) – and coffee shops adopting the frequency model with the 11th coffee being free, for example.

The financial services industry itself is vast and varied, and typically the loyalty space is more complex than retail. Most retail banks reward on spend on the credit and debit card. Credit cards earn more due to available funds through either interchange fees or annual card fee charges. Many retail banks also tier programme rewards depending on how the member engages with the bank. Some may limit this engagement to the number of products held: the more banking products the customer holds, the higher the tier and the higher the earn rate on the card. Other banks create the tiering formula from a combination of transactional and non-transactional behaviours to drive desired activities that will drive card earn rate.

Travel has seen quite a change over the years in terms of how it rewards its loyalty customers. Airline frequent flyer programmes were typically so impossibly complex that no one could easily decipher the traditional 'miles on distance flown' formula. Many airlines have shifted to 'miles on value of air ticket', which feels more equitable to the paying traveller. This is discussed in more detail in chapter 76. Hotels reward either against total spend or on a room stay basis, which definitely feels simpler for the hotel guest: "If you stay with us five times, you can enjoy a free one-night stay experience." This most simply compares to the frequency reward structure at a retailer or restaurant, rather than value-based or distance-based rewards in the airline industry.

Chapter 44

Behaviours to reward: non-transactional

Non-transactional activities are a unique opportunity for brands to engage with loyalty members. If a programme is purely transactional, it feels very much like a contract or, some may say, bribery: "Spend and we will reward you with points or cash back."

Non-transactional activities are often referred to as missions or challenges in loyalty programme communications. Challenges and missions could be refer a friend, update your contact details, write a review, follow the brand on social media, engage with the brand on social media, attend an event, upload a recipe, download the app, turn on app notifications, and the like. This list is endless and can answer many pain points brands would like to solve. Loyalty members often gladly take the opportunity to earn a few extra points or competition entries and the financial trade off is simple. Take, for example, a call centre executing outbound calls to update the critical contact details of a member base. This may cost $10 per outbound call. A simple loyalty challenge to the member may be to update contact details to boost points. The allocated points, as a reward, will cost less than the outbound call costs.

Non-transactional reward structures also allow members to earn rewards quickly, leaving them feeling motivated. If a member is rewarded immediately for sign up and can earn again for answering a quick poll, potentially low loyalty earners can feel the value of their loyalty relationship rather than be demotivated because they simply can't transact at a higher level. The number one reason cited by consumers who don't use rewards programmes is that it takes too long to earn a reward.[32]

> **Rewarding for non-transactional activities helps members feel valued. It is a powerful and meaningful way to keep members engaged beyond the traditional transaction only.**

One brand that has bravely created a loyalty offering firmly on non-transactional and transactional behaviours is Old Mutual, a premium African financial services provider across 14 countries. Old Mutual Rewards incentivises the following behaviours: completing financial assessments to measure financial stress or money personality, attending a short course on moneyversity, signing up to its money management platform, using a savings calculator (for education, retirement, debt relief, income tax and budgeting), completing a survey, and referring a friend. We can see how all of these activities are to the benefit of an individual's financial wellbeing and customers earn Old Mutual Rewards points for completing these activities. These activities are available for points collection even if the rewards member is not yet an Old Mutual customer. However, if the member takes out an Old Mutual product, they are promoted up a tier. This then allows the member to earn more points as a percentage of premiums paid. Points can be redeemed across a multitude of available partners.

Brett Cameron, Managing Director: Old Mutual Rewards states, "Because the financial wellness earn activities aren't limited to our products, we've been able to extend Old Mutual to non-customers as well. When these prospective customers are in the market for an insurance product, they don't just have a positive connection with Old Mutual's brand, they are also better educated about their own financial needs, and much easier to convert in the sales process."

Chapter 45

Perceived rewards value

If there is one key element every loyalty programme manager is aware of it is the power of perceived rewards value. Rarely is the actual value to the customer at the same real cost to the loyalty brand giving away the member rewards. This does not mean that the loyalty brand is being deceitful towards its customers in any way.

Consider the simple loyalty point within a grocery store loyalty programme. Typically, the earn or redemption value may be 1%. When a member has accumulated $20 worth of points, what do they really receive back in rewards value? In the simplest conversion rate, the member may redeem their points for $20 off the next grocery shop. The grocery store may have budgeted for this redemption liability at maximum value (i.e. $20) or at marginal cost (i.e. after cost of sale). If gross margin is estimated at, for example, 40%, then the retailer is effectively paying 60% cost x $20 to the loyalty member, which is $12 rather than full cost of $20. However, not all loyalty operators actually calculate the cost of loyalty in this way.

One of the simplest and most effective ways to offer a higher perceived value of reward than real value is via partnerships. As per the research conducted by Mando-Connect, *What Britons want from loyalty programmes 2.0*, there are numerous ways to increase perceived value, which applies to all industries. The two that stand out with impact are British Gas and Tesco, the latter being well known in the loyalty world. Loyalty giants like Tesco offer three times redemption value at some of their partners versus in store redemption. This offers more value to members but at a lower cost to the loyalty brand.

> **"Forty-seven percent of British Gas customers are interested in holidays, which it does not offer. Partnership with holiday brands enables them to offer more relevant rewards. — Mando-Connect[33]**

An entirely different approach, which we believe adds enormous perceived value to loyalty members, is connected to a brand's loyalty assets. What is a loyalty asset? Something the loyalty brand has up its sleeve that represents more perceived value than any real cost. Let's take the Waitrose sponsorship relationship with the English cricket team. This is the perfect way for Waitrose to connect with its cricket fanatic members. In addition to its main (overt) loyalty value proposition, it can offer either 'meet the players' or 'win access to the English cricket game' at the sacred Lords ground. This sponsorship relationship creates significantly more perceived value than any amount of loyalty rewards in its mainstream value proposition. If they look hard enough, all brands have loyalty assets that add real value, creating higher perceived value than standard rewards.

Chapter 46

Points or cash? Are they the same?

The loyalty point has quite a bad name, which I believe is unjustified. I sit in so many executive meetings where the loyalty strategy is discussed and approved, and too many times I hear the comment, "But we don't want points! Customers don't like points!" We believe passionately that points can play a critical role in a loyalty programme if used correctly and superbly explained to the loyalty member at every step of the loyalty journey.

> **Customer loyalty goes way beyond points but a points based programme is a powerful, tried-and-tested concept for loyalty programme currencies.**

The reason the simple loyalty point is often frowned upon is because it isn't correctly explained. When used in complex programmes, it is almost impossible to calculate how much reward value they have earned due to the deliberate complexity and lack of transparency. This is obviously not what we recommend and I bang the simplicity and transparency drum hard in chapter 27.

The simplest way to ensure that any complexity around points falls away is to state the monetary value of points available in the loyalty account at every single touch point for the member. This needs to be as thorough as when a member logs in to the loyalty portal to check any element of their loyalty account or programme functionality. In addition, monthly loyalty statements need to state the monetary value available and the post transaction message (e.g. via SMS) needs to confirm this balance.

Points will ultimately be redeemed into a benefit to the member that more often than not equals cash, either directly to a member's wallet or off the next purchase or partner spend. Obviously, this list is not exhaustive and there are most definitely broader redemption options.

Every year in the *Truth and BrandMapp Loyalty Whitepaper*, South African consumers vote for 'cash back' or 'points into cash' as their number one preferred benefit. I do not have the same research responses for other markets but the longitudinal study from BrandMapp shows that no matter the demographic profile of the consumer (i.e. income group, age, or gender), all consumers vote for cash back and cash converted from points.

Points also allow the programme operator flexibility if the programme is offering transactional and non-transactional behavioural rewards. Programme managers may wish to incentivise and reward members for updating their cellphone details or social media connections, or the like. A points-based loyalty currency allows members to be rewarded without having to over-reward for ad hoc non-transactional activities that may be worth significantly less than a loyalty transaction on goods or services. In addition, promotional campaigns can incentivise members through double points earned or double redemption value.

Chapter 47

Discounts in store or differential pricing

One of the best known loyalty benefits in grocery retail is discounted pricing for loyalty members on store merchandise. It is certainly not limited to grocery retailing but it does seem to be more common in this industry. I clearly remember a discussion with a retail CEO who said: "Amanda, we need to make the customer feel that it is a no-brainer that they must join our loyalty programme." He also went on to say that they'd be absolutely stupid not to, but let's rather not refer to our customers as stupid!

The obvious upside to offering price differentials in the store is that members immediately receive the programme's benefits. Non-members are faced with a simple decision of join and get the discount or don't join and miss out.

Where this is particularly challenging is when it is not implemented for the right strategic reasons. Such a misalignment on strategy inevitably compromises the customer experience. Too often, such a loyalty benefit is approved with the real hope that suppliers can fund the discounts and unsellable merchandise can be discounted for loyalty members. Let me address each of these points separately, as they both drive a compromised customer experience.

Firstly, if the premise for the discounts is that they must be supplier funded, then the products on offer will be dictated to the loyalty brand by the supplier relationship. The process will not be customer centric and is unlikely to be responsive to the loyalty brand's ultimate drive for personalisation. How can such an approach drive personalisation if the benefits are dictated to the loyalty brand by a 3rd party supplier? I always remember watching prime time TV when a grocery retailer's advert promoted its loyalty programme and what great discounts you could get if you were a member. The problem? The product on offer was the polar opposite in market positioning to the target audience of the prime time TV show. Clearly, it was dictated by a 3rd party supplier funded campaign.

Secondly, let's address offering unsellable items to your loyalty members at a discount. Your most loyal members need more from you than your worst merchandise. If there is plenty else on offer in the loyalty programme, then an extra discount on sale merchandise is acceptable. But, if this becomes one of the only value propositions, then it tells your best customers that you don't care about them. Fashion retailers refer to this marked-down merchandise as the 'dogs'.

> **Discounts in store can add real value if the strategy is customer led. Make sure it is not supplier led and is not driving the removal of 'dogs'!**

I am a big fan of how discounts in store can add real value for the retailer and, of course, for the loyalty member. They can give that feeling of instant gratification and can entice non-members to join the loyalty programme out of FOMO (fear of missing out).

Chapter 48

Personalised covert offers

In chapter 19 we talk about 'The Iceberg Effect', the clearest way to explain the difference between the benefits outlined in the previous chapters and benefits via personalised offers. The two previous chapters refer to overt benefits that are available to all loyalty members against programme rules. A covert benefit is not available to every member in the same format. We know that personalisation creates trust and many previous chapters discuss the positive impact this has for both brand and customer.

Personalised discount vouchers, which are not new, are one way that covert benefits are offered. I like to believe that loyalty operators have perfected the science of personalised offers after the years of Tesco ClubCard pioneering this thinking with Dunnhumby back in 1995. A direct extract from *Scoring Points - How Tesco is winning customer loyalty*, which is a remarkable loyalty book, reads: "When we did our first mailing, and we put the coupon in for money off Coca Cola, we sent it to everyone, and then pensioners and older people started calling saying 'I never buy this, you have to give me offers for something I want'." This highlights the errors Tesco made along its loyalty journey, but as we mentioned before, they were sending personalised mass mailings to millions of members on a quarterly basis virtually from the outset.

> **"Eighty-seven percent of loyalty members reported that they're interested in having various details of their activity watched, monitored, and tracked to receive access to personalised rewards and experiences.**
> **— Bond Brand Loyalty[34]**

Looking at today's retail loyalty promotions, I compared four different member emails received in the same campaign. The products featured in the mailings were different and relevant to each member. Tick!

We must not limit personalised offers to grocery vouchers, although this industry sector has perfected the task at hand. We believe this is mainly due to the granular level of insight acquired through transactional data and, of course, frequency of shop. This does become significantly more challenging for brands with lower frequency purchases. This is where a more diverse level of data points needs to be considered to create a deeper understanding of the member and a better profile to match with relevant offers. Data points like enrolment data, demographic data, social media input, and how a member interacts with your brand can add to the member profile. This is well illustrated by Vodafone, which won awards at The International Loyalty Awards 2020 with the VeryMe programme. It creates over 200 personalised offers a week based on member profiles and how they interact with the brand, in addition to transactional data.

Chapter 49

Always-on benefits

What distinguishes an always-on benefit from points or discounts? And why are they significant in the customer experience which loyalty members crave? An incredible loyalty leader and co-judge at The International Loyalty Awards offers her insight: Cecilia Floridi, Managing Director at DataLab in Germany.

❝ —— Contribution by Cecilia Floridi

We have seen a major shift over the last ten years as loyalty programme providers transition from stand-alone transactions to a more sustainable 'always-on' relationship with customers. The emphasis is now on really understanding target audiences and giving them what they value most throughout their evolving customer journey.

The goal of 'always-on' benefits is to provide ongoing value to members and incentivise them to continue engaging with the brand, no strings attached. Surprisingly, when focusing on specific target groups, benefits that are really meaningful to them tend to be affordable and smart.

Some brands have been pioneers in understanding shifts in customer behaviours to provide customers with exceptional member-only benefits, at no extra cost, in exchange for their data and continued engagement. We are seeing that investments which follow this strategy are showing positive financial results in an increasingly challenging economic climate.

One such example is the UK pet care retailer Pets at Home. It offers free and engaging member-only benefits, which are a key pillar of its loyalty programme. Over 10 million UK pet owners have so far willingly given their personal data during a sign-up process that asks them detailed information about their pets, their home, the animal charities they would like to support as a VIP member, and their preferences.

The programme cleverly understands the structural trend of pet humanisation in the post-pandemic period and draws customers to its VIP Club with an app featuring benefits like help finding a missing pet, upgrades on grooming visits, and discounts on pet insurance policies. Members can donate to their chosen charities after every purchase and select monthly discounts on their favourite pet brands.

Crucially, Pets at Home also aim to lock in relationships with pet owners at the start of their journey and their free VIP Puppy and Kitten Club reflects this.

> “ **You and your Very Important Pet(s) will join over 10 million VIPs and their humans. — Pets at Home[35]**

The retailer´s latest financial results prove that its loyalty strategy is working with healthy growth rates across its key strategic KPIs and customer acquisition metrics. Interim results for 2023 show a significant increase of multi-channel engagement rates and registrations to the Puppy and Kitten Club alone averaging 29,000 per week, more than three-times higher than pre-pandemic levels.

”

Chapter 50

By invitation only

There are certain tools in a loyalty manager's tool box that really are reserved for the best customers. One of these is referred to as 'by invitation only' (shortened to BIO). If more programmes adopted such strategies, the overall member experience across the industry would be elevated. The use of BIO activities for members can hardly fail, if executed well.

BIO experiences can either be overt or covert. In overt propositions, the loyalty brand shows all members that such a highly sought-after tier exists and labels it clearly 'by invitation only'. MYER one, the multiple award-winning programme for Australia's department store Myer, offers a tiered programme with its Platinum tier clearly 'by invitation only'. Previously, the Platinum tier used to state 'by invitation only' but left the actual value proposition empty. I love this concept! It created intrigue and mystery. However, I am sure there are grounded commercial reasons why this strategy has changed.

MYER one tiers

Another loyalty proposition very close to my heart is the British Airways Executive Club Premier card. I am not supposed to have favourites but will share a personal story to showcase how this tier is used by British Airways. Like most airlines, BA doesn't disclose the path to its VIP status – Premier. Benefits include being able to book seats on flights that are already full and access to The Concorde Room at Heathrow, to name just two. It also gives the personal cellphone number of each country's General Manager so Premier passengers can always access the most senior BA executive in that country. As the General Manager of British Airways in South Africa, I had the pleasure of meeting Premier members. I personally had the privilege of offering Nelson Mandela a Premier card; he graciously accepted the VIP status. I was naturally starstruck as he towered over me (he was 1.93m tall) in the first class cabin, amusingly, with holes in his socks. The BA Executive Club Premier card isn't a covert proposition but the airline certainly doesn't promote Premier as an overt tier, making it semi-covert.

The use of covert 'by invitation only' experiences is extremely powerful. As we discussed in chapter 34, a segmented approach to member communications and loyalty experiences will offer greater member satisfaction. We encourage loyalty brands to identify their loyalty assets and use these as offers and incentives for top customers through a segmented approach. Imagine taking your best customers to Château de Saran, an estate that is the centrepiece of the Moët & Chandon empire.

> **“You cannot pay to come and stay. You have to be asked.**
> **— Stephane Baschiera, ex CEO Moët & Chandon[36]**

Loyalty members would forever remember such an experience, especially as money cannot buy it. What are your loyalty assets and how can they create unforgettable 'by invitation only' memories?

Chapter 51

Surprise and delight

Surprise and delight is very similar to 'by invitation only' from the previous chapter. They definitely overlap but, in this case, all activities are covert. There are no overt tiers; otherwise we would lose the surprise element.

> **Fifty-eight percent of consumers indicated that the most important way a brand can interact with them is through surprise offers and gifts. — Merkle[37]**

There is no question that members love to receive surprise-and-delight moments from their loyalty brand. I mean, who wouldn't? I have said from my earliest loyalty days that a simple phone call to our top customers would go further than a bunch of points. Around the leadership table of the British Airways South African team, we would take the list of top Executive Club members and allocate, for example, five members each per week to call. The response was overwhelming. Fast forward a couple of decades and the same strategy still has impact. At Truth, we worked with IBL, one of our clients in Mauritius, to launch the award winning wiiv Rewards programme. The wiiv call centre staff deliver outbound calls to wish top members 'Happy Birthday!' Cécile Henry, Group Loyalty Manager, confirmed that members couldn't believe that wiiv took time to wish them happy birthday, and post-call engagements reached a phenomenal +458% increase.

For the most loyal members, it is unlikely that such strategies will increase spend as they are possibly already at maximum wallet share, but it has been proven to reduce churn. Holding on to top customers is paramount. However, Ellipsis concluded that not all customers respond equally to surprise-and-delight campaigns. The most loyal customers love being rewarded in this way but less engaged customers may view such offers with suspicion and could defect completely.

There are different ways to offer surprise-and-delight gifts. One most obvious choice is to surprise customers on their birthday. Last year, my regular online grocery shop with Checkers Sixty60 did just that by placing a surprise chocolate bar in my delivery to wish me 'Happy Birthday!' I have no doubt that it was supplier funded but I didn't care. I was delighted and here I am telling all the *Blind Loyalty* readers about the experience, so it clearly created advocacy. Antavo suggests adding extra surprise by offering the unpredictability of celebrating a member's half birthday.

The Australian beauty brand Mecca has created its Mecca Beauty Loop programme around a series of surprise gifts. It is a tiered programme based on spend levels. The surprise gift will change depending on the member's tier but the broader offering consists of a birthday box, the Beauty Loop box, and bonus boxes. Depending on tier, members receive between four and nine boxes per year (once they have reached level one, which has a minimum spend threshold). This programme does challenge my opening paragraph stating surprise-and-delight strategies are covert; the Mecca Beauty Loop programme overtly states its membership offers surprise boxes depending on tier status.

Chapter 52

Softer benefits: soft but impactful

Let's not assume that softer benefits mean softer impact. I would argue that the softer benefits will yield greater emotional loyalty than the traditional earn against transactional activities. Softer benefits often come as part of a higher tier status, but not always. The most effective way to explain softer benefits is to showcase brands that skip around the outskirts of transactional rewards and yet delightfully engage members with softer benefits.

> **Softer benefits offer members more meaningful and longer lasting memories than traditional transactional earn exchanges.**

Let's start with some real programme examples. Ikea offers a 60-minute childcare facility at its stores while customers shop. Members of the Ikea Family loyalty programme can take advantage of an additional 30 minutes of childcare at the same stores. I don't know about you but I have never managed to navigate my way around an Ikea store in less than 60 minutes so this additional softer benefit would have been a huge win for me when my kids were young.

Keeping within the homeware category, Restoration Hardware offers softer benefits like a complimentary interior design service or concierge service to manage the order process. These benefits are completely on brand and relevant to RH's members.

The fashion industry is known for offering exclusive member only events for higher tier members. Such events are an opportunity to showcase new product launches and entice members with a glass of champagne. In my experience, such events yield positive sales results. Not only do they show positive sales results on the evening but they also offer a longer 'stickiness' impact, i.e. customers who attend and purchase at a member-only launch continue to show a higher engagement rate after the event. In addition, fashion retailers often include a tailoring service for alterations as part of the softer benefit set offered to members.

There has been no shortage of airline examples throughout this book because airlines continued prominence in the world of loyalty is no secret. Simple benefits like a chauffeur drive to the airport or even to the aircraft door are available for top customers. This is over and above the benefits most frequent flyers take as everyday programme advantages, like priority check in or lounge access.

Lastly, we look at the beauty industry, which lends itself to a more emotional connection with its members. One of my favourite simple examples is Sephora's Beauty Insider – Rouge tier (top tier), which offers members first access to products. This makes Sephora's top customers feel special and offers an immediate feedback loop.

Chapter 53

Redemption options: points into prizes

Loyalty programme benefits can be as varied as your imagination allows. Different programmes have different ways of earning a loyalty currency and a variety of redemption options. Remember that not all programmes work only with an earn-and-redemption (burn) currency; some programmes use earn-and-burn mechanics coupled with other programme benefits. This chapter is dedicated to redemption options.

Traditionally, loyalty currencies can be redeemed into a cash value to be used either in the loyalty brand itself, at a partner as cash value against goods and services, or as direct cash back into the member's wallet.

The ability to redeem outside of the traditional cash equivalent options mentioned above has become more prevalent in so many programmes. Partners can offer a vast array of redemption choices and experiences and these are often provided behind the scenes by an aggregator of merchants across a variety of industries. This means that a loyalty member's loyalty currency can be redeemed, for example, against grocery shopping, travel, cash value at a partner retailer, restaurant meals, fuel, or leisure options like spa days or kids' entertainment. Obviously, what is available for redemption should depend on customer profiles and redemption behaviours.

> **Redemption into travel, merchandise, or experiences is what the loyalty member remembers more than how they earned loyalty points.**

Financial service companies can add variety, with points becoming a currency for investment or payment of banking fees. Points across all industries can be used as charitable donations, which shows what role the loyalty programme can play in a brand's higher purpose. We cover this in later chapters to ensure it is thoroughly explored. Sharing points is also a compelling proposition for loyalty members who wish to pay it forward.

Whether or not a programme has a points or cash currency, lifestyle options are becoming more popular as part of programme value propositions. Lifestyle options can include some of the partner rewards mentioned earlier, like spa experiences or family days out. There are providers to loyalty programmes that also offer educational or career courses, hobbies, children's education, or professional development. This is becoming more and more popular. According to Johan Moolman, former CEO eBucks (judged as the best long-term programme at The International Loyalty Awards in 2023), 47% of eBucks customer app interactions are on loyalty value propositions like education, security, online books, and the like. Since the pandemic, app-based solutions for exercise are available for either the yoga bunny or marathon runner and can add real value to your members. Points can be redeemed against monthly subscriptions or the loyalty brand can itself offer the subscription as a value-add to its members.

Chapter 54

Does redemption really change behaviour?

Many loyalty professionals who have been in the industry for years may remember the days when breakage was ideal. What does this mean? Breakage is the non-redemption of loyalty currencies and it creates a perceived cost savings against issued points not redeemed. However, this creates a liability on the company's balance sheet, which is explored in detail in chapter 95.

The loyalty world has thankfully moved on; breakage is no longer encouraged and redemption is often seen as a strong indicator of true customer engagement. I had the pleasure of listening to The Loyalty Podcast, hosted by Iain Pringle (episode #7 in 2020). The insights from the discussion between Iain and his guests are really powerful and worth sharing.

❝ —— Contribution by The Loyalty Podcast

The podcast initiated a great debate about whether or not redemption was good. I can't help but agree with those who believe redemption is a good thing. Customers change behaviour mainly after a redemption experience. Dave Canty spoke about how jetBlue TrueBlue members increased their interest and uptake in the airline co-brand card offering post redemption compared with control groups. David Feldman cited performance statistics from Qantas that showed that the greater the number of miles redeemed in the redemption transaction, the higher the likelihood of that member repeating flight bookings on Qantas.

Staying with the theme of airline and travel redemptions, Iain Pringle shared that after redeeming points for flights in the Avios programme, members were more likely to continue to collect (earn) Avios. However, other lower value redemptions via partners tended to have the opposite effect. Iain refers to the 'cashing out' effect: earning just enough for the smaller reward, i.e. cashing out, and then not returning to use the brand for further earn transactions. However, overall, he did state that redeemers perform better than non-redeemers.

A lot of people spend time focusing on the earn but the real change of behaviour comes from the redemption. — Phil Gunter

There is most definitely a human psychology angle at play; as members approach a redemption threshold, they accelerate earn behaviour. Immediately after the redemption, earn levels go down again but often to a higher level than pre-redemption rates.

Iain debates the difference between savers and spenders in loyalty programmes; these two types of behaviours for redemption can often be the same person behaving differently in different types of loyalty programmes.

In the *Truth and BrandMapp Loyalty Whitepaper 2022*, we definitely saw some customers stating that they wanted to be instantly rewarded for their brand loyalty while others shared that they like to build up for big rewards. In addition, an equal number of customers said they want both! These are the most demanding customers in terms of what they expect from loyalty programmes.

Chapter 55

Redemption experience

Throughout the book I refer to customer experience and its importance to the overall loyalty experience. The redemption process is no different and, if I need to exaggerate anything for any part of the loyalty journey, the redemption touch point is it. Way too many brands fall into the trap of placing less focus and, dare I say, less importance on the redemption experience.

> **Redemption should be as natural as buying behaviour; therefore, excel in your user experience.**
> **— Andre Larisma, ex CEO Sanlam Reality[38]**

My preferred ecommerce brands allow me to buy my chosen merchandise at the touch of one or two clicks. Redemption should be the same and I see this in my favourite loyalty programmes, which I use daily. These allow me to redeem my banking loyalty currency in its associated partner network as easily as any credit card payment. This is a real win, showing deep integration of loyalty partners and eliminating all friction from this quick redemption transaction. This encourages me to keep earning more of the currency as it is so easy to redeem and so utterly satisfying to receive free goods.

Let's think back to the earlier loyalty years. I remember my dad buying fuel from the local Shell garage. He'd collect his stamps on a stamp card and, when the card was full, he could choose from a catalogue of available goodies. How quickly he could receive the goods was questionable. As the promotions advanced (and I stress the word promotions here, as these formed the basis of some loyalty structures, which we call loyalty programmes today), the process seemed to get simpler.

I recently had the pleasure of working for a client in Africa. To prepare ourselves, we did a market map through mystery shopping at competitor merchants. Only a year or so ago, retailers were requiring loyalty members to make a trip to the store to select a chosen gift for redemption. Once chosen, the customer would disappear for one week and then return to collect the gift from the store. This highlights the unexciting and intensely laborious process to redeem some loyalty points.

The overall redemption experience is obviously dictated by seamless technology application. Real-time capability is required to ensure that points and rewards earned in one loyalty moment must be available for redemption at the next (no matter how soon after the first loyalty transaction takes place).

I'd much prefer to click click or tap tap to receive the full value of my hard-earned redemption reward, either in the loyalty app or on a partner's website. I may even prefer to swipe to push my available reward value into my digital wallet to share with my kids or donate to charity. One step too many and I zone out.

Chapter 56

Programme rules and the BRD!

One of the painstaking activities before launching a programme is teasing out each of the programme rules. It is likely that the commercial earn and redemption rules will be tackled first but the details behind tier rules and points expiry, for example, are also critical and commercially sensitive. The next few chapters are dedicated to discussing the major programme rules of auto-enrolment or opt-in, tiering, and points expiry.

Most loyalty technology vendors have a process to capture all the required input data that enables all details of the programme to be finalised; technology will be built according to these exact specifications. I think it is worth discussing the Business Requirement Document, affectionately known as the BRD. Most loyalty programme managers shudder at this three letter acronym as it requires such an intense level of detail after hours and hours of workshop interactions. What does the BRD cover? In a nutshell, it must contain every single element of the programme capability. It must also state what is out of scope so that the business is clear about what are day one launch requirements versus potential future requirements on the programme roadmap.

Programme rules, which do not have their own dedicated chapter, are worth a mention on the next page, given they could dominate 50% of the BRD preparation time for business teams and technical teams alike.

Can you imagine the level of detail required to understand the programme rules about permission fields for communication opt-in, as the first example? In a world of strict data legislation, this cannot be misunderstood or incorrectly applied. Is the member opting in to the loyalty programme communications only, or to broader brand communications? Which channel? Does the programme offer permissions by channel? If the company is a service-orientated brand, like a sports club, it may need to send operational communications such as 'the water supply is interrupted so there are no shower facilities; please use an alternative club.' Does the loyalty programme or the operating brand have permission to send this?

> **The BRD, an infamous three letter acronym, sends shivers up the spines of business teams, and yet it is one of the most essential documents for every loyalty team.**

The BRD will obviously outline in detail the earn and redemption rules. In doing so, it will need to outline the customer experience by activity and by channel. This all underlines our earlier theories around the importance of customer service in the overall loyalty experience and redemption customer journey. The BRD can assist all loyalty programme managers to get this right. Which channels will be used and what will the user journeys per channel be? This must be set out for every single activity that a member will undertake in the programme. This thought process must go beyond the fun part of a loyalty programme (i.e. earn-and-burn activities) and also cover the mundane elements, like enrolment and customer service. How does a member access their account? What if they lose their login password?

Fasten your seatbelts and enjoy the BRD ride! You cant avoid it (if you want a decent loyalty programme) so rather embrace it.

Chapter 57

Auto enrol or opt in? Is it even a question?

One would think that with today's data legislation this isn't even a question but interestingly, it still needs to be discussed. Why? Some products or services can lend themselves to encompassing the loyalty proposition as core to their customer value proposition and not as an additional opt in.

The lines between product and loyalty in financial services are often blurred. Let's discuss an example of an insurance product in the banking suite of products. By taking out the insurance policy, after three years of on-time premium payments and zero defaults, the customer will automatically receive 25% back off its fourth-year premium. Is this a product incentive or a loyalty incentive – and how do they differ? Do they even need to be differentiated? This example, the 25% premium reduction is an incentive for tenure (three years of product holding) and positive payment behaviours (non-transactional activity), both of which are often elements of a good loyalty programme. The insured customer didn't opt in to a separate loyalty initiative when taking out the insurance policy; it was automatically included with the customer's benefits. This may be an extreme illustration but other products and services can veer towards such a structure; the loyalty brand needs to be crystal clear if it requires a separate loyalty opt in.

Another much debated scenario for auto enrolment is when a programme is relaunched. Does the loyalty brand auto enrol existing members from the old programme into the new? There may be a vastly different value proposition with new terms and conditions. Legally (although each country has its own legislation, so this is not necessarily a global standard), the programme operator should be able to auto enrol all existing members into the new programme as long as they have effectively communicated the changes within required timescales, for example a 30-day notice period. In particular, this communication is essential if there are any changes to the value of the loyalty currency or even a hard stop for redemptions. The existing members need to be forewarned if the future redesign won't allow existing balances to be redeemed and given time to do their redemptions.

Regardless of the above examples, there are commercial considerations of auto enrol and opt in. An auto-enrol scenario offers maximum membership base and no drop-off from unread communications. Considering that email open rates are unlikely to be higher than 20–30% (best case scenario), one can immediately calculate campaign performance rates, i.e. campaigns to encourage opt in. On the flip side, however, if members haven't consciously opted-in for the incentive or the full loyalty programme, they may be completely oblivious of the loyalty programme and the brand may end up paying for zero change in behaviour.

> **Opt-in enrolment drives a conscious mindset for members joining a loyalty programme.**

This is always the concern when calculating programme performance. How much of this tracked behaviour would have happened anyway without the cost of the incentive? If customers have consciously opted in, they are more likely to be motivated to change behaviour. This is not forgetting, of course, that the programme will engage frequently and meaningfully with its members to remind them of the programme benefits and required activities (transactional and non-transactional).

Chapter 58

Points expiry – is it really necessary?

If there is one way to get a member agitated and expressive about how they feel about their loyalty membership, it is to expire their points.

> **Points that do not expire result in happy members and a higher customer lifetime value.**
> **— Len Llaguno, Managing Partner KYROS[39]**

Why would a loyalty programme operator consider expiring points? It may initially seem simple. Once a point is issued, it sits as a liability on the company's balance sheet until it is used or expired, i.e. until it is no longer available to yield value to the member. This whole subject is expertly explained in chapter 95 by Len Llaguno, our contributor on liability.

There is no question: if points are expired, the member experience is severely compromised. One third of consumers state: "I hate it when my points expire before I can use them," according to the *2022 Truth and BrandMapp Loyalty Whitepaper*.

Let's review how brands address this critical programme design element, starting with first prize from a customer experience point of view: no expiration of points. This is becoming more regular in programme rules but not regular enough, in my opinion. As examples, Virgin Red do not expire points; jetBlue TrueBlue frequent flyer points never expire.

An alternative approach is to expire points only if there is no activity from the member. For example, Etihad Airways Guest Miles do not expire as long as there is activity within 18 months. Activity is defined as earning, redeeming, or buying miles to name a selection of valid behaviours. Other airlines follow the same structure but some have more generous periods of 36 months, for example, Iberia Plus and British Airways Executive Club for Avios. Retailers often use this formula of expiring points after inactivity only. Therefore, if members are shopping or redeeming points, their points won't expire. Typically, due to higher frequency of transactions than airlines, retailers use a 12-month inactive period as the programme rule.

Some loyalty programmes still expire points after a period of time post issue. The retail industry usually uses 12 months although some extend to 24 or 36 months. The airline industry is usually 36 months. Both Turkish Airlines and Singapore Airlines operate with a 36-month expiry period after miles issue and no activities will extend the validity of these miles. However, members can pay a fee to extend mileage. Airlines also use their co-branded credit card activity as an incentive to keep miles valid.

Other initiatives that brands use to potentially expire points are activities like forcing a voucher issuance on reaching a threshold of points and attaching a validity period (for example three months) to the voucher. I personally don't like this approach, as it takes away the customer's choice as to when they may wish to use points. Remember chapter 54 where we highlighted the fact that different customers prefer to spend points, save points, or often a combination of both. In Vodacom's VodaBucks programme, members need to 'bank' issued points once a month to move earned points into their VodaBucks account. This adds friction to the experience but after banking points, members are more engaged at a higher level.

Chapter 59

To tier or not to tier?

Tiered programmes do have a place in the world of loyalty. However, this doesn't mean that every programme should be tiered. Often there are brands that would potentially do more damage to their brand positioning by tiering a loyalty programme. Jean Tranter from TFG Rewards, a multi-partner programme with 30 million members, stated that tiering is not beneficial for The Foschini Group customers.

> **"Some customers already feel like they are in the lowest tier in life; you don't need to tell them they are on the lowest tier in your programme. — Jean Tranter, Head Credit Risk and Product Foschini[40]**

As is the case with so many concepts in the loyalty industry, airlines pioneered programme tiers from the outset. Tiering allows airlines to offer higher elite status to frequent flyers, offering service elements like lounge access, priority boarding, and other VIP experiences, that make a frequent flyer's life more pleasant. Without doubt, these VIP experiences mean more than the mileage currency collected in the member's account. Hotels have followed the airline industry model and clearly differentiate member benefits and service levels by tier. Higher tiers enjoy early check in, late checkout, free wifi, and the like. It is impossible to offer such VIP treatment to all customers; tiering creates a simple and effective solution.

Certain brands lend themselves to tier structures more easily than others (unlike TFG Rewards). Harrods has a tiered programme that is completely on brand and makes sense to members. Many of the North American department stores also operate brilliant tiered programmes, with clear benefits for the higher tiers like tailoring services or the choice of your discount day. Higher tiers may also offer higher base earn rates on every transaction.

The financial services industry offers tiering to change banking and insurance behaviours. Members are incentivised to earn higher credit or debit card rewards according to their tier. Higher tier status is achieved through, for example, higher product holding in the bank or insurer, or by completing relevant activities that serve both the member and the financial institution (see chapter 44 – non-transactional activities). The Discovery Vitality programme is a well-known brand in the healthcare industry, with over 40-million members in 40 countries worldwide. It is a tiered programme, with Diamond being its top tier. Celeste Williams, Head of Marketing for Vitality South Africa, says: "Diamond Vitality Health Clients spend 40% more on healthy food than Blue Vitality Health Clients."

In chapter 19 we introduced the concept of overt and covert value propositions using 'The Iceberg Effect'. Overt and covert tiers should be managed by programme managers. The overt tiers are available for all members to understand and aspire to by completing activities that are overtly stated. Covertly, loyalty programme managers should be taking members on a segmented (tiered) journey with personalised experiences relevant to that segment (tier). (See chapter 34.)

The loyalty industry cannot all be wrong. Tiering does play a role in enhancing the customer experience and assisting loyalty brands to achieve a positive ROI. According to Antavo's *Global Customer Loyalty Report 2022*, "Organisations with a loyalty programme that includes tiers reported a 1.8x higher return on investment compared to those which don't offer tiers."

Chapter 60

Sustainability: does it really matter?

There is no question that customers are showing value-based purchasing behaviour and expressing a preference for brands to help them by asking questions like is the brand greener, ethically better, or respecting privacy laws? At the Comarch User Group in September 2022, Thomas Husson from Forrester expressed the unavoidable tension between what consumers say they will do and what they actually do. It is a challenge to convert attitude into actual behaviour. Barriers like cost, convenience, time, performance of products, knowledge about and trust of the right product choice all challenge consumers to follow through with what they want to do versus what they actually do in purchasing value-based products or services.

This is where loyalty programmes can play a critical role in successfully incentivising such behaviours. Decathlon Decat Club offers 4,000 points for planting trees or beach cleaning. What stands out from Decathlon's insight is that only 13% of Club members actually donated, but those who did are 10 years younger than the average member, indicating that the younger generation is more mindful and focused on a value-based choice.

We particularly enjoy the insights derived from Mando-Connect's research with YouGov in Great Britain, which quantifies how improving sustainability in loyalty marketing is a majority, not a minority issue. Charlie Hills, MD and Head of Strategy at Mando-Connect, offers impactful insight into this subject.

“ —— Contribution by Charlie Hills

Sustainability matters. Gro Harlem Brundtland, the Chair of the Brundtland Commission, defined a sustainable development as “one that meets the needs of the present without compromising the ability of future generations to meet their own needs.” The need to protect our world should be top of the agenda.

And yet, in loyalty marketing, it rarely is. How many programmes can genuinely say that they think about their impact on future generations in their strategic planning? The majority prioritise customer, brand, and business metrics. Few and far between are the programmes operating to a genuine sustainability agenda.

> “ **Sustainability in loyalty is the engagement of the customer base in a responsible and sustainable way — Charlie Hills[41]**

Seventy one percent of Brits think loyalty programmes should help people live more sustainably or support the environment. The most appealing things that programmes can do to achieve this are: reward members for sustainable behaviours (44%), offer rewards to help people live more sustainably (43%), support environmental causes (39%), offer rewards from brands that support sustainable causes (33%), offer a digital card (31%), and offset their carbon (28%).[42]

There are some really valuable case studies of programmes operating one or more of these tactics - from global programmes like H&M Membership, which rewards customers for bringing their own shopping bag or donating used garments, or Lidl Plus, which only offers a digital card, to market specific programmes like M&S Sparks, which supports environmental charities. Without question, programmes can and should improve their sustainability impact.

—————— ”

Chapter 61

Loyalty and the environment – a perfect mix!

This is possibly one of the easiest chapters to write as the industry is awash with amazing examples of how brands are using their loyalty programmes to step forward and do the responsible thing. But before we showcase the world's best environmental loyalty examples, is it even worth it in terms of effort on the part of the operating loyalty brand? It is absolutely worth it as customers expect the loyalty brand to care about the environment and to do something about saving the planet. In fact, they are basing their loyalty choice on such actions.

> **Sixty-five percent of 18–34 year old customers consider 'environmental protection' matters in their loyalty decision. — Loyalty Science Lab[43]**

Patagonia is probably the world's most famous brand in terms of care for the environment. Patagonia states that 'earth is its only shareholder'. For this reason alone, the Patagonia brand manages to harness more brand loyalty than any other loyalty programme initiative. They offer store credit for recycled clothing and believe passionately that they build deeper customer loyalty by building trust because their business stands for something.

Foot Locker is a well-known global brand that allows its loyalty members to donate Foot Locker loyalty points for activities like carbon credit offsets, restoring biodiversity, beach cleaning, and habitat preservation for flora and fauna. In the previous chapter we quoted the Decathlon Decat Club, which rewards environmental activities with points. Foot Locker, on the other hand, encourages redemption of its loyalty currency into environmental causes, which is a more common loyalty practice. Both Foot Locker and Decathlon are brands working with Allcolibri, a technology provider that enables brands to empower their customers to make a real social and ecological impact.

Internationally celebrated loyalty programme MySchool MyVillage MyPlanet created the MyPlanet proposition to respond to environmental causes. This programme encourages members to shop at multiple merchants and a percentage of spend is allocated to chosen beneficiaries. MyPlanet allocates funds to provide training to support biodynamic farming in Southern Africa, as one example.

In Indonesia, global giant Coca Cola launched Recycle Me Rewards to reduce plastic waste in Indonesia. Members are incentivised to recycle PET bottles and receive reward points. Bizarrely, however, this isn't an 'always-on' initiative, but a repeated tactical campaign.

Etihad Airways has gone one step further, offering its green loyalty programme Conscious Choices to both passengers and businesses. Corporate customers can earn rewards for carbon offsets, investment in sustainable aviation fuel, and paying a fuel surcharge. Etihad intends to achieve net zero emissions by 2050.

According to *The Loyalty Magazine 2023 Awards Winners edition*, Adidas adiClub promotes 'noble causes' and, by tracking its members running 56 million kilometres, Adidas has cleaned up 500,000 pounds of plastic waste. It has fully integrated its loyalty programme into the business's core focus on sustainability via a circular 'buy, use, recycle, re-use' chain.

Chapter 62

Social loyalty – a thing of the past or future?

Loyalty programme managers love the idea of loyalty members engaging frequently on social media and posting glorious reviews of the loyalty programme through the various social channels. In chapter 44 we review non-transactional activities and mention that following brands on social media and engaging with them via social channels can earn members additional points through identified missions or challenges.

> **Customers interacting on social channels, sharing their reviews and pictures of their experiences, are strengthening their bond with your brand, plus they're encouraging others to try your brand. — Annex Cloud[44]**

Many years ago, Bain & Company published statistics showing that engaged customers spend more: "Customers who engage with companies over social media spend 20% to 40% more money with those companies than other customers." They showed that this is even true for engaged 'detractors' from NPS (Net Promotor Score), who also spent 20% more. 'Passives' spent 30% more and 'promotors' spent 40% more, once engaged. The fact that even 'detractors' once engaged are spending 20% more is most significant.

The Bain & Company statistic is matched by thousands of other survey results showing the impact of social media on positive buying behaviours. I am most interested in the data impact of a social loyalty strategy. If executed well, a social loyalty strategy can harness the loyalty brand with more insightful data. It becomes a marriage between traditional transactional data and social data. By combining social data like consumers' social influence, brand affiliation (taken from 'likes' and 'follows' of competitor brands), and other demographic insights, loyalty campaigns could become so much more impactful. The loyalty member will enjoy the interactions more due to the hyper personalisation and campaign results should yield incremental performance.

Here are a few examples of brands executing interesting social loyalty propositions. My Lancôme Rewards offers rewards for members connecting on multiple social channels. Purchases with a brand like Lancôme are certainly influenced by customer advocacy and so its integration of loyalty and social media channels really makes sense. As far as we can tell, few financial services brands seem to enter into social loyalty. However, Standard Bank's UCount programme has incentivised Twitter activity for years.

Standard Bank Twitter and Instagram rewards

Chapter 63

Web 3.0: how can loyalty adopt the craze?

Firstly, it is worth defining what web 3.0 encompasses. I simply interpret it to include cryptocurrencies, the metaverse, and NFTs. These remain a mystery to some and fully adopted by others. It is still early days so, no matter what loyalty strategy a business follows, it will need to be aware that segments of its customer base will willingly engage while others will be sceptical, ill informed, and unlikely to engage. At the Comarch User Group 2022, Laura Ducournau from Velvet Consulting said that growth statistics show a higher adoption rate of NFTs, crypto trading, and metaverse engagement year on year.

Early adopting brands like Starbucks, Burger King, and Club Paris St Germain already use cryptocurrencies within their loyalty value propositions. Before brands launch into deeper investment, it is worth measuring whether consumers wish loyalty brands to adopt such benefits.

Thirty-eight percent of consumers report the availability of digital collectibles and NFTs to have an impact on their loyalty decisions.
— Loyalty Science Lab[45]

In addition, the younger consumer is more likely to engage with the metaverse: "More than half (57%) of the consumers under the age of 44 consider the availability of metaverse brand interactions impactful to their loyalty decisions."[46]

Some brands have made positive inroads. I'll start with Lacoste and its launch of web 3.0 UNDW3 loyalty programme. Card holders can accrue exclusive rewards by solving quests linked to Lacoste's history and engaging with Lacoste. The Lacoste UNDW3 card's ultimate aim is to co-create its brand of tomorrow. The more members engage in the community, the more decision-making power they have in the future of the brand. They earn points that are displayed on the site's leaderboard. The card itself is a dynamic NFT, allowing card holders to purchase limited edition merchandise and access physical events, like Roland Garros.

Starbucks is mentioned as an early loyalty adopter in the block-chain and NFT community. It launched its Odyssey Rewards for members to engage in Odyssey Journeys and collect digital stamps (NFTs). Odyssey Journeys include activities like a virtual tour of a Starbucks coffee farm in Costa Rica, or interactive games. The NFTs become a currency to unlock Starbucks experiences that are not available anywhere else. Such experiences include a virtual espresso-martini making class and highest level rewards like a trip to the Costa Rica Starbucks coffee farm.

Unfortunately, it is too early to share the commercial performance of such loyalty initiatives. Watch this space! More and more brands will integrate web 3.0 into their core loyalty programme in fascinating ways.

Chapter 64

Child's play or serious strategy: Gamification?

I have lost count of the number of times boardroom executives roll their eyes when the word 'gamification' is mentioned in the context of loyalty. It is deeply misunderstood and the potential positive impact on customer loyalty massively under-estimated. Glenn Gillis from Sea Monster explains why and makes a powerful case for the need for gamification to sit at the heart of a loyalty play.

“ —— Contribution by Glenn Gillis

A game can be defined as an activity that has a goal, rules, feedback, and, critically, voluntary participation. Gamification is applying these ideas, and others from game design, to non-game contexts. Both can be useful to the next generation of loyalty schemes.

> “ **Games are a natural fit within the marketing mix in order to equip brands to thrive in the dynamic landscape of customer loyalty. — Glenn Gillis**

In the context of loyalty, what is the goal? On the one hand, we need to ask, what is the company's goal? I would suggest it's recognising the lifetime value of a customer and offering them more than just a product at discounted prices, moving beyond reward schemes and really deepening that engagement with the customer. On the other hand, we need to ask, what is the customer's goal? Ultimately, a customer wants to feel connected to a brand, which means that they want to be seen and recognised as more than just a basket of goods, an upsell opportunity, or a transaction.

When we consider what the rules might be in this exchange, in most loyalty schemes the rules are complicated. They involve customers choosing to buy one product over another (usually at a discount) or doing other activities on the off chance that they might win something based entirely on luck. Within a quality game, typically, the rules are simple and clearly understood by everyone. Within a loyalty programme, the rules should be that active engagement is rewarded in order to build a relationship with their chosen brand.

As regards feedback, games are particularly good at balancing boredom and frustration. They are also very good at providing visual feedback using playful design that allows you to know exactly where you are and what needs to be done next. So, are your customers' rewards statement visual, with clear feedback that shows what the next best action is, or simply a set of numbers, tiers, or whatever?

And lastly and most importantly is the voluntary participation piece where people want to be rewarded for their time and engagement, not just for the transaction they make. And they do not want to be shouted at or have their social or entertainment experiences interrupted by a brand. Rather, they want value added and that's what a game does - it exchanges value for time. Brands that engage with their customers in a space that is relevant and authentic to them will succeed. Whether it is light gamification on the one side or something with much more depth, borrowing from these same principles and applying them to how your brand is going to show up authentically using games or game principles will ultimately boost loyalty in the short term, and increase life-time value in the long term, without having to constantly pay customers to engage.

——————————— ”

Chapter 65

Payment-linked loyalty

Payment-linked loyalty is, as the name suggests, the link between loyalty identification, payment, and loyalty earn. For the consumer, it is a completely seamless process of payment (as normal) and earn, as participating loyalty programmes are embedded into the transaction. Loyalty benefits are automatically allocated to members' accounts from data gathered during the payment process.

There is an enormous data benefit of such capability. The payment-linked loyalty provider can harness aggregated data to offer insight into transactional behaviours across different merchants and help drive more effective campaigns, with focused personalisation, in the future.

The industry has already seen complete integration between in-store digital experience, payment, and loyalty through brand apps. The QSR industry (quick service restaurants – see chapter 78), in particular, is no stranger to such innovation, enabling order ahead, skip the queue, payment, and loyalty in one tap of the phone. There is no question that technology capabilities make this easy for merchants and customers: "Creating a new paradigm that is set to revolutionalise the whole industry, Coinbridge seamlessly merges loyalty and payments into one." – Guy Rosenhoiz, CEO Nayax Coinbridge.[47]

Enterprise loyalty brands may present different challenges. There is brand value in the loyalty brand they have created and app space on a phone or card space in a wallet is 'loyalty real estate'. Such retailers, or other merchants, want some disruption for their members to remind them of the benefits of the loyalty programme. If such a process means the loyalty swipe becomes invisible, will members be as conscious of the programme as they are today when the shop assistant asks for their loyalty card or app? Conscious loyalty customers will change their behaviour more so than unconscious members. We see Woolworths Everyday Rewards in Australia showcase its approach to payment-linked loyalty in its Everyday Rewards app. Members link a preferred payment card and simply pay and earn points via a QR scan at check out.

> **“ Eliminating the friction normally associated with in-store loyalty results in much greater levels of customer engagement, with typical campaign participation levels of 70–90%. — Payment Loyalty[48]**

Co-branded FFP credit cards seem like an original version of payment-linked loyalty and programmes like Air France / KLM Flying Blue and Emirates Skywards have recently launched payment-linked loyalty across their merchant partners.

Emcan, Emarat's 2023-launched fuel rewards programme in the UAE, has coined the phrase 'Limitless Possibilities'. In doing so, its next innovation release will be NPR: number plate recognition. This will enable payment and loyalty rewards processing, simply by driving onto the forecourt of an Emarat fuel station, which leap-frogs payment-linked loyalty, as we know it today.[49]

The frictionless experience still remains utopia – the whole loyalty industry must strive to ensure the customer experience is as seamless as possible. There is no question that payment-linked loyalty enables a frictionless loyalty and transaction experience; and the battle of 'loyalty real estate' must play out in this not-so-new technology.

Chapter 66

Omnichannel loyalty

There is simply nothing more frustrating than not receiving the same loyalty experience across different channels of a brand. As a consultant in the industry, it is easy for me to understand why this may be the case, but, as a consumer, it is simply irritating. As a loyalty professional, it is quite obvious that such challenges come about due to technology roadmaps and internal prioritisation by companies.

The simplest way to describe this practically is that a loyalty programme is launched against an agreed internal project date but not all customer channels are aligned in the same roadmap. This could mean that some of the customer channels will only be integrated into the loyalty programme months later. The negative impact on the customer of anything other than a fully positive omnichannel experience is inevitable.

Let's take a fashion retailer programme, which operates via store, website, and app commerce. The programme offering is discounts on selected merchandise and ad hoc personalised vouchers. From the outset, the discounts are applicable through all channels, which is favourable for the customer. However, the personalised vouchers are only redeemable in store. This is a typical shortfall in technology capability behind the scenes, which will not be tolerated by savvy and engaged customers. They are more connected than ever and expect their favourite brands (including the loyalty proposition) to meet their needs across all channels.

Dr Melanie Van Rooy is Marketing Director of Clicks, which is the largest pharmaceutical chain in South Africa. The Clicks ClubCard programme is the most used loyalty programme in the country, with 79% of South Africans using one of the country's oldest loyalty offerings. Dr Van Rooy is clear that an omnichannel customer is a significantly more engaged customer with the Clicks brand.

> **Our loyalty members who interact with us via the Clicks app spend 3.7 times more than an average customer. — Dr. Melanie Van Rooy, Marketing Director Clicks**[50]

Forrester states that, "15% increase in customer retention is typical for retailers that implement omnichannel loyalty programmes." There is no question that customers who use more channels are more valuable overall.

Source: Marketoonist.com

Chapter 67

Is it old fashioned to want a loyalty card?

Traditionally, loyalty programmes were geared around a card: 'swipe your card', 'what colour is your card?' Has the industry moved on, or is there still a place for the loyalty card? I genuinely believe the answer is market- and industry specific.

The airline industry has completely transformed from frequent flyers traditionally carrying their airline loyalty card that granted access to the prestigious lounge and priority check in. Today, all frequent flyer benefits are available through showing an app that clearly shows tier status and associated benefits. One would imagine, therefore, that loyalty members have moved on and now prefer digital solutions. It remains a mystery to me that some markets still clearly show that consumers want a traditional loyalty card, either for status or possibly because of a distrust of digital alternatives.

In most retail stores, there is a full suite of digital and analogue loyalty options available: app, card, WhatsApp, QR code in a cellphone e-wallet, multi-tenanted card app, or simply just a cellphone number. The digitally savvy amongst us may not understand that some consumers genuinely wish to swipe a traditional loyalty card, given that there are so many alternatives available. If we think about payment-linked loyalty from chapter 65 and less integrated options, why take out a plastic card?

The role of WhatsApp in loyalty has grown exponentially in recent years. Even if it's less valid as a loyalty identifier, it can serve the loyalty industry in different ways. WhatsApp has become both a service channel for loyalty programmes to reduce call centre costs and an engagement channel. Clickatell, a global chat commerce platform, confirmed that a grocery retailer was able to reduce its call centre calls by 50% after implementing a WhatsApp bot to help manage blocked card queries. – Werner Lindemann, SVP: Global Sales, Clickatell.

> **There's something nostalgic about swiping my loyalty card. Call me old-fashioned but it holds an element of prestige.**

Some markets will obviously penetrate app usage more than others. It is important to remember that consumers may wish to limit the volume of apps, not necessarily due to data usage but rather due to phone storage capability. That is definitely a restriction in lower income markets. I know that I don't want an app for every brand I interact with. If I refer back to chapter 18, where we discuss loyalty promiscuity, I imagine the exact same principles apply to app usage. Consumers will choose the brands they most wish to interact with, rather than a 'free for all' mentality of downloading every app available. In order for a brand to increase engagement, how useful is the app? How integrated is the loyalty experience? How much extra value does this app add to my everyday life? If the responses to each of these questions is positive, then app adoption and loyalty engagement will be positive.

Section 3

Industry excellence

Chapter 68

The fuel sector is no novice in the loyalty industry

If ever there was a loyalty industry sector with too many world-class examples to name them all, it's the fuel industry. It is incredibly competitive and really drives amazing innovation. We all know that fuel is a grudge purchase for most of us, so hats off to the industry for continuously driving innovation through loyalty propositions around the globe.

Firstly, does loyalty make the same impact on the commercial results of the fuel company as other industries? It would be wrong to say it does, because it is well known that the number one driver of forecourt choice is location. Drivers are unlikely to go far out of their way to fill up with fuel. However, if there are two fuel brands equidistant from the driver, loyalty will most definitely play its part. Whilst world class retailers may boast that about 80% of revenue is through the loyalty card, fuel brands tend to achieve lower revenue penetration.

> **We often saw loyalty programme transactions accounting for 50% of total fuel sales (and sometimes as much as 70%). — Pawel Dziadkowiew, former BP Loyalty Manager[51]**

Fuel sales penetration varies as an average across developed and developing markets: 50–70% sales penetration for developing countries and 25–40% for developed markets.[51]

In his interview with Let's Talk Loyalty, former Shell Executive Pavel Los said that loyalty members at Shell spend between four and five times more than non-loyalty members. Obviously, within this statistic, there is a strong bias of 'member self-selection' (i.e. best customers will join the loyalty programme), but it is nevertheless an impressive loyalty KPI.

Let's examine the vast array of loyalty propositions used in this highly competitive industry. There are obviously traditional earn-and-redeem programmes, based on transactional behaviour. It is imperative that this also includes spend in the convenience store and other non-fuel purchases, like the car wash. In addition, immediate real-time earn-and-redemption capability is required so members can earn at the pump and redeem those points in the convenience store. Some markets are restricted by fuel discounting legislation and to circumnavigate this, fuel is often a significant partner in other loyalty propositions, like banking and retail, or a key player in a coalition loyalty programme.

I believe that the fuel loyalty programme can add immense value to the overall brand experience, more so than in other industries. Customers can better keep track of this grudge purchase through the loyalty app via monthly digital receipts. Payment processes can also be simplified through the loyalty app, enabling members to experience payment-linked loyalty at the fuel pump. BPme Rewards has placed emphasis on how its fully integrated loyalty app vastly improves the brand's customer experience offering.

One of the more innovative programme propositions is Circle K's Play or Park programme. Members earn points on transactional activities (on fuel, convenience, and non-fuel) and points can be 'played' or 'parked' monthly. The monthly play enters members into a draw for exclusive experiences like a trip to the Grand Prix, New York shopping trip with friends, or a car. The more a member transacts, the more 'plays' they have. Members who play receive a monthly treat like a coffee, pastry, or free car wash to say thank you and encourage future engagement.

Chapter 69

Watch out retail: FMCG loyalty is real

The overarching challenge for FMCG – Fast Moving Consumer Goods – or CPG – Consumer Packaged Goods – is that, more often than not, the company doesn't own the relationship with the consumer. Traditionally, retailers held this trump card via their traditional retail loyalty programmes and the FMCG brands fell in line with the retailers' programmes. But times have most certainly changed and many FMCG brands have successfully managed to change this scenario to own this primary relationship and gather zero and first party data.

In order to understand this subject better, let's hear from an inspirational marketer who was in the deep end of this fascinating industry. Sadika Fakir, former Integrated Media and Digital Director at Tiger Brands South Africa, gave us this perspective on FMCG loyalty marketing. Tiger Brands is woven into South African society. Over 100 years old, the company manages an expansive portfolio of South Africa's favourite brands.

“ —— Contribution by Sadika Fakir

CRM and loyalty in any category exists to build deeper relationships and engagement with consumers. This is no different in consumer goods. Whilst consumers rely heavily on the rewards and loyalty programmes of retailers where consumer goods are sold, there is still an open opportunity for consumer goods to build deeper relationships and engagement with their consumers.

In a tough economic landscape, consumers seek more value from the brands they support otherwise they will turn to the dealer-owned brand or value-for-money competitors; brand loyalty is being challenged in these times.

Achieving sustainable growth and long-term brand relevancy starts with getting to know our consumers, serving them contextually relevant and personalised communications, and incentivising their loyalty.

It has to go deeper than just transactions, though. CRM and loyalty provide platforms for surveys, competitions, inspiration, and two-way conversations with consumers, allowing for consumer goods companies to understand not just purchase patterns but rather a complete view of consumer and their preferences.

> **"Eighty-nine percent of US consumers will reveal purchase intent and other preference data if you offer a value exchange. — Cheetah Digital[52]"**

There are some outstanding examples of FMCG loyalty programmes where brands have managed to secure direct relationships with their consumers due to meaningful value exchanges. Some stand-out examples are Kelloggs Family Rewards, Lancôme Elite Rewards, and Pampers Club. Alternatively, there are programme operators that offer rewards to consumers by collating rewards and cash back from FMCG brands and bypassing retailers to incentivise shopping choices. Snapnsave is a successful example of this.

Chapter 70

Grocery retail: Go big or go home!

Grocery retail is one of, if not the, most competitive sector, and adding loyalty into the mix makes it even more exciting. With or without loyalty, there is fierce competition and a laser-like focus on price comparisons. Loyalty programmes can fundamentally aid price perception but programme operators need to be aware that much cynicism exists with regards to loyalty programmes masking hidden prices to offer the perception of better value. Do not fall into this trap; ensure that your pricing strategy is not leaving consumers confused. Obviously, in a covert manner, retailers will offer varied promotions and relevant offers on price to segments of customers via a personalised strategy and approach.

There is only one way to truly understand grocery retail and that is to talk to a grocery retailer who has spent her career in loyalty and personalised communications. Melissa Hanley is from Pick n Pay, a major retailer in Africa. Pick n Pay launched the first of many retail programmes in South Africa, with Smart Shopper.

“ —— Contribution by Melissa Hanley

Retail grocery loyalty programmes benefit both retailers and customers, and finding the balance between the two is complex and challenging. Retailers gain access to valuable customer data and shopping behaviour patterns that set the scene for an improved shopping experience, be it with an optimised range, enhanced service, or targeted promotional offers. In return for sharing their data or buying into promotions, customers are rewarded for their loyalty with targeted offers, discounts, or cash back. If executed effectively, a loyalty programme should be a win-win for both the retailer and the customer.

Finding the balance – and win-win scenario – can be complex, especially in a struggling market. Increasingly, customers are becoming 'loyal to the deal' as they scan retail leaflets in search of the best deal to stretch their budgets instead of being 'loyal to the card'. This is driving margin pressures for retailers as they seek to offer the most attractive offers to retain market share. This fragmented spending affects the value perception of a loyalty programme. Customers benefit less on any one programme and instead see smaller benefit scattered across a few loyalty cards. This results in a lose-lose situation as both parties are compelled to invest more effort to find great deals to suit household budgets.

The grocery retail loyalty landscape and customer needs have fundamentally shifted in recent years but this provides an exciting opportunity to reinvent grocery retail loyalty offerings so that the benefits remain relevant to customers.

Earlier in the book, we assessed different programme structures and benefits. Grocery loyalty programmes around the world have tried and tested all options. It feels like the more recent launches are more likely to consider a no-points approach with innovative ideas, like the 2022 launch from Asda, with Asda Rewards. Rather than points, consumers complete shopping or activity missions to build up a cash pot.

A loyalty programme should be saying thank you to our customers, rather than expecting them to say thank you to us. — Matt McLellan, VP Customer Planning & Proposition Asda[53]

Chapter 71

Fashion – dreams dressed in retail loyalty

Loyalty is deeply embedded in the fashion industry and not a new concept. The sector is awash with brilliant, relevant loyalty concepts; in fact, it's a playground for innovation. I mean, who doesn't want to engage with fashion?

> **Clothes aren't going to change the world. The woman who wears them will. — Anne Klein[54]**

Classic earn-and-redeem programmes are basic and boring in fashion. We expect more and the industry sector gives us more. What resonates in fashion are eco-rewards, non-transactional behavioural rewards, and tiering.

Eco-friendly fashion brands that stand out are H&M and Patagonia, which encourage recycling of clothes for sustainable fashion. Sports brands (which are arguably becoming more like fashion retailers) are punching above their weight in terms of using the loyalty proposition to encourage a change of behaviour. In earlier chapters, we referred to Decathlon, the French retailer that encourages member participation in eco-friendly events by rewarding them with loyalty points. We also showcased adidas and its sustainability play via the adiClub, which encourages members to track running mileage to clear plastic waste; in return, this leads to sustainable footwear.

Non-transactional rewards are well documented in chapter 44. Some industry sectors lend themselves to really excel in this area;

fashion is one of them. The Vans shoe brand created a D2C (direct to consumer) strategy and Vans Family played its part, harnessing non-transactional rewards for over 12-million members. Vans Family members get rewarded for transactional spend, but also for engaging with the brand by, for example, uploading content with Vans shoes on social channels. Many fashion brands encourage social engagement and reward via the loyalty programme. Other activities that can be rewarded are writing a review, uploading fashion photos, referring a friend, and the like.

Tiering has a key role to play in fashion loyalty to allow for enhanced rewards or top member experiences. In chapter 59, we showcased the MYER one Platinum tier, which offers 'by invitation only' top-tier experiences like private shopping evenings at the store for friends. So many fashion stores run tier-based programmes where the benefits increase by tier, like earn rate, shipping costs and speed of delivery, extra benefits such as shopping days, magazines, complimentary alterations, and free parking.

Benefits	Silver	Gold	Platinum
Point Ranges	0-99 points	100-199 points	200 and over
MyModanisa Welcome Points	5		
Profile Confirmation: D.O.B	2	2	2
Points Earned From Reviews	2	2	2
Birthday Points	3	5	10

Benefits	Silver	Gold	Platinum
Free Shipping		Orders over 50 USD	All orders
Gift Points Benefit (Extra 1 point)		Every 5 points	Every 3 points
Be Informed About Special Offers and Deals	✓	✓	✓
Benefiting From Discounts with Priority			✓
Invites to Special Events			✓

Modanisa is a three-tiered fashion loyalty programme; its tier benefits are shown here. Most fascinatingly, according to Antavo, its loyalty technology partner, the top tier members, Platinum, have an eight-fold higher frequency than Silver members, and a seven-fold overall customer spend level versus Silver members. This is a strong case study of the impact of tiers in the fashion industry. Again, let's not forget that some of these results will have the impact of member self-selection built into the results quoted.

Modanisa tier benefits - Antavo

Chapter 72

Everything has beauty, especially a loyalty programme

There are some strong parallels between the fashion industry and the beauty industry in terms of their loyalty programme raison d'être. Some similarities are rewarding deeply for engagement rather than purely on spend and using the power of tiers in the loyalty proposition. Both offers are used by most beauty brands' loyalty managers.

Potentially, one major difference in the two industries is channel strategy. Some beauty brands are retailers and hence they can create the direct customer relationship through traditional retail loyalty activities. However, many beauty brands are manufacturers needing to create a connection with end users. They need to create a D2C (direct-to-consumer) channel; loyalty plays an impactful role for these brands.

> **We believe creating authentic and meaningful relationships that are engaging translates to love and long-term loyalty. — Kelly Mahoney, VP Customer Marketing Ulta Beauty[55]**

In addition, loyalty can assist in influencing many different players in the beauty industry ecosystem. Brands will wish to influence the end user or consumer, shop assistants in retail stores (either their own branded store or a third party retail partner), and beauty therapists.

The role of social influence is paramount in the beauty industry. We discussed how Lancôme uses rewards for social media engagement in its D2C My Lancôme Rewards programme.

The overall power of creating a direct relationship with the end user is well illustrated by the beauty brands that have combined the loyalty proposition into a customer engagement tool. Activities like virtual consultations, digital colour matching for make up, or digital skin analysis all lead to better insight for the beauty brand to better service their customers. Ultimately, this will lead to increased sales and customer retention. Without a hook like a loyalty programme, how do many of these brands create that coveted connection with end users that can open the pathway directly to offer additional, virtual services, as an example?

Globally, there are many impressive loyalty brands in the beauty industry. However, if I had to choose the one most highly regarded in the loyalty profession, I believe it is Sephora. It states that 80% of its revenue is through the Sephora Beauty Insider programme, with 17-million active members. It is a three-tier programme: Insider, VIB (Very Important Beauty), and Rouge tiers. Its benefits set is clearly split into three offerings: 'savings', 'samples', and 'experiences'. 'Savings' offers monetary value back via points earned and redeemed, free shipping, seasonal savings events, point multiplier events, 5% off subscription or replenishment purchases, and end of year discounts. There are additional elements to the 'savings' proposition for Rouge tier only. 'Samples' are offered as a birthday gift and higher tiers offer exclusive gifts and the Rewards Bazaar (for which Sephora Beauty Insider programme has become famous). Finally, its 'experiences' offer covers access to same day unlimited delivery, app exclusives, and exclusive events like free facials, meet and greet famous brand owners, and product master classes. Overall, the Beauty Insider programme is structured simply and offers clear value across the three pillars of 'savings', 'samples', and 'experiences'. The actual experience itself is sprinkled with elements of gamification and, of course, personalised offers.

Chapter 73

Retail banking: rewards or loyalty?

Bank-wide loyalty programmes are particularly difficult to execute. They need involvement, buy in and execution across multiple and diverse business units within the bank. David Parker, Chairperson of the judging panel for The International Loyalty Awards,[56] gave the example of a retailer running its loyalty programme but also managing other diverse business such as a spa, car rental firm and a garden centre. More and more successful banking loyalty programmes are tackling the bank-wide approach successfully. Two brands that stand out strongly are Avion Rewards from Royal Bank of Canada and eBucks Rewards from First National Bank, South Africa. The real insight into retail banking for this chapter is from Johan Moolman, former CEO of eBucks Rewards, the only company to win three awards at the 2023 International Loyalty Awards.

" —— Contribution by Johan Moolman

eBucks Rewards is 23 years old and has given away more than 20 billion rand since inception, which is approximately $1 billion. Annually, in recent years, we have given away over $100 million per annum. eBucks is a tier-based programme and we track and reward against 10 different behavioural categories. We actually operate nine different programmes to address demographic sub- segmentation within our country but customers only operate within their own relevant programme, based on their transactional banking product.

We are a programme for everybody, meaning we offer eBucks rewards to all customers from the lowest income customer to the wealthiest banking client.

> **“ Rewards programmes have just become so much more important in helping customers get through the month, and many customers are actually budgeting on their rewards. — Johan Moolman**

It is our duty to help customers and, in order to do so, it needs to be a collective effort of the bank i.e. transact, credit, invest, insure, car and home financing, and so on. The more our customers interact with us with transactional and non-transactional behaviours, the more they earn. The money has to come from somewhere; $100m per annum is paid out against behavioural changes. This is why we call it a rewards programme (rather than a loyalty programme). We want our customers to become financially fit and able to retire when they need to; we reward customers for taking these steps with us.

Ninety percent of our eBucks are redeemed in the first 30 days of members receiving them. This is possible because of the partnership network we have with the best of category brands, plus our own ecommerce store and travel platform. There is something for everyone to redeem into whether it's to make the monthly budget stretch or to book flight tickets for vacation. Members can also enjoy lifestyle benefits such as education, security and gaming offers. Forty-seven percent of our 300m unique app interactions have engaged with these recently added benefits in the past 12 months. Clearly, this is an appreciated benefit.

eBucks is steadfast in its belief that it is only successful if the customer wins, our partners win, and the bank (FNB) wins. All three stakeholders must benefit.

”

Chapter 74

Telco: engaging gargantuan customer volumes

In an industry fighting for customer retention, a loyalty programme can create a positive excuse for customer engagement. The permanent threat of contract changes can be overcome with a loyalty relationship.

There are a few global examples of telco brands that seem to be getting it right. In fact, the brands that seem to be doing it well year on year are Turkcel from Turkey, Telus Rewards from Canadian company Telus, Priority from the UK's O2, and VeryMe Rewards from Vodafone UK. I am personally drawn to VeryMe Rewards as Vodafone has shown how to present personalised rewards at scale, using transactional and engagement data to do so. In addition, the VeryMe Rewards proposition has been recognised as an award-winning proposition in both the B2C and B2B sector.

To share a telco loyalty case study, we hear from Mateboho Malope, Group Loyalty Executive Vodacom Group.

“ —— Contribution by Mateboho Malope

Unlike many other service providers and retailers, very little information is known to us about our customers, making tailor-made offers, personalisation, and relevance – all of which make customers feel valued – a huge challenge. Inevitably, loyalty programmes in the telecommunications industry are very much transactional and less likely to capture customers' hearts.

Despite mobile operators investing heavily in rewarding and retaining customers, the multiplicity of standalone efforts – such as targeted promotions and campaign messages – has failed in delivering the meaningful interaction that we strive for.

Vodacom reimagined and reinvented its loyalty offering by introducing a single value proposition that intends not only to reward its customers, but to build a more engaging relationship with them. — Mateboho Malope

The VodaBucks Rewards Programme is free to join, available on three different customer platforms, and now has more than 26-million opted-in customers. In addition to a daily free rewards, customers can earn the virtual currency that is VodaBucks through the things that they already do such as mobile spend, and by achieving personalised behavioural goals. Earned and banked VodaBucks can be redeemed for airtime and data bundles, a wide range of offers in the Vodacom e-commerce platforms, donated towards a good cause, and, as of October 2022, converted into cash! Through this inclusive model, we deliver significant value not only for our customers but also for our partners and Vodacom itself.

VodaBucks is now crossing borders and scaling into the rest of Africa. For the first time, customers in international markets will be able to earn and spend VodaBucks on what they wish, when they wish, as they wish.

”

Chapter 75

Travel and hotel rewards

Everyone loves to travel so this is an industry consumers run towards more easily than less exciting grudge industries, like insurance. Plus, it is easier to create a higher perceived value to the consumer in travel programmes. There are so many incredible examples of world-class hotel programmes, but I want to start the chapter with Mastercard Priceless.

Mastercard Priceless is a credit card offering, and the benefits are travel and experiences. Experiences vary from a yoga class while sailing around the Statue of Liberty to a guided tour of an ancient city. I love the way a single offering can open up a world of choice for customers. This isn't a traditional loyalty programme; it is a side benefit of the financial product. But, without question, it will create loyalty to the product and brand. Access to Priceless is straightforward as long as the customer has a Mastercard product.

The broader OTA (online travel agent) industry is definitely not short of loyalty programmes. The largest OTA, Booking.com operates a tiered programme, triggering discounts when you reach Genius tier one (out of three tiers). Its main competitor Expedia.com, has launched One Key across three of its brands: Expedia, Hotels.com, and Vrbo. One Key is also a tiered programme, offering 2% earn on car rental, hotels, and packages, with flight bookings earning 0.2%. This will generate OneKeyCash to spend on future bookings.

Similar to the airline industry, we see that hotel loyalty members' revenue contribution (for the well established brands, like Marriott Bonvoy and Hilton Honors) is approximately half of the room nights booked. Another travel industry similarity is that the hotel loyalty programmes' points tend to expire after a given period. However, expiry is often easily extended if the member is active, or if elite status is achieved. Out of all the world's biggest programmes, I believe that only the Best Western Rewards programme's points don't expire. Another parallel feature of the hotel and airline industry is lifetime status. According to Rob Burgess in his daily email, *Head for Points* on 16 July 2023, only three hotel loyalty brands offer lifetime status: World of Hyatt, Marriott Bonvoy, and Hilton Honors. The estimated hotel spend to achieve lifetime status is approximately $200,000.

I am most impressed by the award-winning GHA (Global Hotel Alliance) Discovery programme. GHA is the world's largest alliance of independent hotels. Its core programme allows loyalty points to be earned and redeemed across hotels, golf courses, spas, and restaurants. What impresses me is that GHA Discovery members are offered VIP recognition at any of the 800+ hotels, even if they are not staying at the hotel. By virtue of their GHA Discovery membership, members can access facilities like golf courses, the spa, and the pool. The alliance also offers hundreds of small independent properties access to a global loyalty programme and its members which they wouldn't otherwise reach.

I recently heard a quote that resonated with me, from Mehdi Hemici, Accor Hotels, "Loyalty is not a destination; it's a customer journey."[57] Accor Hotels has received feedback (in the quotation below) from their Live Limitless members, which we believe should become the mantra for all loyalty professionals:

> **"Make my life simple, make my life special, and look after me — Mehdi Hemici[57]**

Chapter 76

An industry shift from the traditional FFP

Given that so many of us refer back to the airline industry as the foundation for modern day loyalty programmes, this chapter is bursting with insights to share. Why? Not only because FFPs (frequent flyer programmes) started the loyalty trend in the early 80s, but also because the industry has undergone such rapid change. The loyalty industry in airlines is now almost unrecognisable from what it was in pre-pandemic years.

First and foremost, before we unpack some of the major industry changes, being part of an FFP gives travellers a sense of security.

> **When I fly with an airline whose loyalty programme I don't belong to, I'm just 30% more nervous the day before I fly. — Rory Sutherland, Vice Chairman Ogilvy[58]**

This level of trust and security is worth its weight in gold but is clearly only achieved through a solid loyalty offering that has not failed its members. This means it offers benefits like tier status or miles earned and when the rubber hits the road, the FFP has purpose from a customer service point of view.

Overall, most airlines have simplified their formulae for earning miles, if not also tier status. This simplification has seen some shift from distance-based formulae to a simpler revenue-based approach. Neverthless, tier status and bonus rewards still keep us on our toes in terms of completely understanding the entire industry, which has traditionally been overly complex.

Airlines have showcased their ability to offer real personalisation. Cathay Pacific has taken its business class experience to the next level: "The airline is logging the travel habits of lucrative business-class flyers, such as their wanting their seat laid flat, in a bid to individually tailor flights for them."[59] Emirates Skywards, with over 32 million[60] FFP members, tailors its email campaigns on data insight on tier status, points available, and interaction with programme partners. This approach yields 86 different variants of personalised communications per campaign.

One of the major shifts the industry has seen is the role FFPs are now playing beyond flight rewards. So much so, it's actually incorrect to still label them as frequent flyer programmes. American Airlines' AAdvantage no longer labels itself as an airline programme. The AAdvantage tier system recognises status through flights, co-brand card spend, and spend with other merchants: restaurants, retail, and so on. A similar approach has been taken by IAG Loyalty from IAG (International Airlines group, home of British Airways, Iberia, Aer Lingus, Level, and Vueling airlines). The Avios currency has over 40 million collectors worldwide and over 1500 merchants to create a loyalty network of everyday lifestyle brands. This refined approach to loyalty is summarised by Rob McDonald, Chief Commercial Officer for IAG Loyalty.

❝ —— Contribution by Rob McDonald

Loyalty programmes have never been so important! I believe we are entering a 'golden age' for loyalty where many brands and companies have moved it right to the top of their agenda. I'm seeing more and more brands using the loyalty lever – from coffee to trainers, from the high street to streaming services – all competing in the same space. As a result of this, these brands need to either create a strong emotional pull or a distinctive offer, or they need to re-think customer loyalty.

—————————— ❞

Chapter 77

Airline loyalty: when some parts are more than the sum

This chapter is not about the sector of airline loyalty programmes but about the remarkable commercial value created within and by FFPs. Evert de Boer is one of if not the world's leading expert in airline valuations; he generously contributes to the understanding of this complex yet fascinating subject. Evert is Managing Partner at On Point Loyalty and CEO of Fidivio.

❝ —— Contribution by Evert de Boer

From their humble beginnings as gimmicky marketing tools, frequent flyer programmes have transformed into financial powerhouses. The most recent example of this occurred in 2020 when US carriers did not resort to the tried-and-tested approach of preselling of miles to partners but instead opted to collateralise the future cashflows from their programmes. The resulting transactions produced not only some of the largest ever financial market transactions for airlines ($9 billion in Delta's case), they also pulled the curtain on the remarkable value attached to the airline loyalty programmes. AAdvantage and MileagePlus, according to their projected values, were significantly more valuable than the respective airlines as measured by their market capitalisation at the time.

Loyalty businesses are essentially considered to be more stable and profitable compared to the airline business. Airlines compete with a commoditised product leading to a historical financial performance where the return on invested capital (ROIC) hardly exceeds the weighted average cost of capital (WACC). Loyalty programmes, on the other hand, offer very different characteristics. In many ways they are, when considered on their own merits, a different business altogether. Arguably, loyalty programmes are more akin to digital innovators like Uber and Airbnb rather than their core airline counterparts.

Some US carriers' projected FFP values are significantly more valuable than the respective airlines. — Evert de Boer

In simple terms, the main operational benefits of airline loyalty programmes result in the cash generated by the spread on points, interest on negative working capital requirements, and the breakage revenue. In addition, this activity does not require substantial investments so there are low cash outflows related to capital expenditures. As a result, loyalty programmes receive different levels of valuations from very different types of investors compared to those investing in the core airline industry.

The most successful programmes are characterised by a very strong customer value proposition. But played well, they can deliver incremental value beyond engendering customer loyalty. A well-run and well-structured loyalty programme can be priceless for any airline.

”

Chapter 78

Quick Service Restaurants: loyalty is king in QSR

We have seen an explosion in the QSR (quick service restaurants) industry and their impactful loyalty propositions. We have deep insight offered below by Ros Netto, Head of Loyalty for leading QSR brand, Kauai. Before we delve into the leading health and fresh QSR offering by Kauai, I want to share KFC Rewards Arcade's launch story. It has shaken the industry by removing loyalty currency from its programme and offering customers the chance to win free food every time they order at KFC. The in-app experience delivers triggered journeys and has resulted in +44% increase in daily app users and +22% increase in weekly app transactions. KFC Rewards Arcade is the 2023 winner of best loyalty initiative for leisure, experience, and entertainment at The International Loyalty Awards.

“ —— Contribution by Ros Netto

The Quick Service Restaurant (QSR) industry, as its name suggests, is all about speed of service and delivering a convenient ordering experience to help customers get what they want when they want it. This was prevalent in years preceding the COVID-19 pandemic, however, over the last few years (post pandemic), we've seen an acceleration globally of digitisation in this space. This sector has enabled experiences for customers that recognise them for their patronage no matter where or how the customer decides to order from them (from their app in the comfort of their home, on the go, 3rd party delivery apps, or physically in store).

QSR loyalty programmes are typically characterised by a hybrid model encompassing a combination of instant gratification reward mechanics coupled with experiential rewards in the form of tiering. Big global hitters such as Starbucks and Chipotle have spearheaded this space through rapidly adopting a digital first experience typically characterised by a strong loyalty programme that is fully integrated into the core functionality of the ordering experience.

Since our first store opening in 1994, loyalty has always played an important role in the way in which we recognise and reward our customers for their patronage. At Kauai, we believe that a loyalty programme should go beyond offering just cash back and points. In our world, a loyalty programme must encompass the value of the reward on offer together with a seamless customer experience. The combination of these two factors determines the true value exchange between Kauai and our customers to foster a long-term relationship.

> **Our most engaged customers yield up to quadruple the average basket than less engaged or non-loyalty members. — Ros Netto**

The Kauai loyalty programme offers customers an immediate 2% cash back reward on all purchases, ticking the box for instant gratification. When customers order ahead, order for delivery, or pay with the app in store, this cash back is automatically allocated to their Kauai wallet balance; for purchases in our stores, customers can also scan the app to earn their cash back. When customers choose to redeem their cash back or vouchers is entirely up to them, so the combination of automatic redemption of vouchers or self-selection is key to enhancing the customers' experience, and is noted as one of the most important factors our customers rate as part of their love for our loyalty programme. The programme also features a tiered loyalty structure, which differentially rewards very loyal customers and allows us to personalise their experience based on their behaviour within the programme.

Chapter 79

Positive behavioural change in the wellness industry

Globally, there is one stand-out brand in the wellness industry that highlights how a formalised approach to behavioural change can benefit both the consumer and the organisation and drive positive outcomes for all stakeholders. This is Discovery Vitality. Founded in South Africa, Discovery is now a global enterprise in the financial services industry. Its approach to rewards is its Vitality programme. The company operates off a shared value model, meaning that the members benefit, Discovery benefits, and society at large will benefit. Celeste Williams, Head of Marketing South Africa for Vitality, gives us incredible insight into Discovery Vitality.

“ —— Contribution by Celeste Williams

Discovery Vitality was founded in South Africa 26 years ago, as a behaviour-change programme. Today, the Vitality platform exists in 40 markets around the world due to its success in helping people live longer, happier, healthier (and rewarded) lives.

Discovery Vitality's aim, executed through its successful model, is to help members change their behaviour for the better, to improve their overall wellness, and to encourage and entrench these behaviours by giving members some of the richest rewards in the financial services, health, and travel industries globally.

When Vitality members do regular health screenings, keep active, drive well, and spend money responsibly, they are rewarded – and well. This good behaviour and healthy habits add up to rewards like massive travel benefit (flight discounts and holidays), top-of-the-range electronics (like iPhones and Apple Watches), shopping and entertainment spoils, and not forgetting hundreds of coffees and smoothies. But the actual reward is their improved health and wellbeing.

> **Our most engaged members on the Diamond status had 81% lower risk of death during COVID-19. — Celeste Williams**

For instance, research has shown that, during the COVID-19 pandemic, those who engaged in healthy behaviour continued to be rewarded, but also had better health outcomes, avoiding severe illness, hospitalisation, and even death. This true reward keeps our members fiercely loyal - and living longer, healthier, and happier lives.

If we look beyond Discovery Vitality, gym loyalty and rewards programmes are very common globally. It is well known that retention in fitness clubs is extremely challenging; as quickly as new members sign up in January each year, non-engaged members leave. A loyalty programme can help reduce attrition significantly to incentivise frequency of visit, duration of workout, cross functional use of facilities, value-added service usage (like personal trainers and sports massages), and consuming healthy food options. Gamification can run wild in such loyalty programmes to keep members engaged, motivated, and competitive with each other and themselves. Successful programmes also create a broader ecosystem of adjacent partners which add value to members via discounts or incentives for sports equipment, healthy eating, and healthier lifestyle (see chapter 98 – for the Virgin Active example). Interestingly, all of this is actually captured within the Vitality programme.

Chapter 80

B2B loyalty: the same or different?

When your customers are businesses rather than individual consumers, there will most certainly be different dynamics to consider in designing and running an appropriate loyalty programme. There are some exceptional examples globally of loyalty programmes delivering value in B2B, for example, IBM – Know your IBM, which has been a multiple awards winner at The International Loyalty Awards.

There is no one better placed than Mark Maclure from Stream Loyalty to unpack whether B2B loyalty is the same or different compared to approaches required for traditional consumer-led programmes.

❝ —— Contribution by Mark Maclure

The world of B2B is very different from B2C for a number of reasons; a company's client base will be varied and consist of multiple customer types who will, very likely, need to be approached in differing ways. This client base will be smaller in number than consumer programmes but significantly higher value, so the need to segment and target them differently becomes crucial. A B2B business may also have multiple routes to market and therefore different channels and partners with whom – and through whom – they transact. There is also a big difference in the customer relationship. In B2B the relationship is (obviously) a business one and it is often the case that you have multiple different contacts. One or some of those contacts within a business suddenly change as staff move and you are left engaging with a new stakeholder.

There are a lot of transferable elements from B2C that will work in B2B (after all, we are humans and therefore all consumers!) — Mark Maclure

As a result, the concepts of engagement and reward work as motivators, but it is important that you consider what will work for each segment. The Pareto law is much more prevalent in B2B so high value customers are even more valuable and will need a very different strategy and programme compared to the large pool of other customers. More flexibility and scope is required, with the ability to dial activities up and down becoming even more important, like having the ability to run targeted 'campaign-based' loyalty is important.

B2B loyalty may also include the ability to reward actions and behaviours rather than purely transactional activity. In addition, deciding what rewards you can offer to customers may be more complex. You will need to consider any sector-related restrictions or regulatory barriers that may exist. Rewards could easily be your own products or services but you may also need to provide only business-related rewards or even include charity donations.

In short, there is no catch-all – loyalty in B2B has complexity but, deployed well, the results can be superb.

Section 4

Launching and managing a programme

Chapter 81

Programme launch – implementation project planning

Every loyalty project is different and requires a different route to launch. However, this chapter offers guidance for most project teams to create and run a programme launch. It is broken down into seven high-level steps.

1

PROJECT MANAGEMENT

- Identify the key project team members across the various organisational teams. These become the working group members who meet weekly and make things happen.
- Identify steerco members, who are key decision makers; they meet monthly to sign off strategic decisions and progress.
- Manage the project plan, resolve queries, and create monthly reporting of progress against the plan and approved budget.
- Manage the RFP if an external loyalty vendor is required (see chapter 88).

2

MARKETING

- Create all elements of customer marketing collateral: brochure, card, website, app, social media, and even above-the-line creative work.
- Create a through-the-line media plan (with agency).

- Write FAQs (frequently asked questions), Ts&Cs (terms and conditions), and privacy policy; work with the legal team for sign off.
- Create a comprehensive member engagement plan (see chapter 29).
- If required, plan the migration of the existing loyalty base onto the new programme. Ensure that legal timelines are adhered to regarding notification periods for programme changes (often 30 days).

3

IT

- If using an external vendor, select the loyalty vendor as part of the broader IT team.
- If it is an internal build, create and manage the IT team.
- Map out customer journeys with the marketing teams to ensure alignment from the programme design into the customer experience.
- Create a BRD (business requirements document – see chapter 56) and, ultimately, an SSD (systems specifications document).
- Ensure that customer service channels are in scope.

4

PEOPLE

- Create training materials with the marketing team and plan training sessions [may need TTT (train the trainer) for large staff volumes].
- Work with senior management to ensure customer KPIs are built into the leadership KPI structure.
- Create an internal communications plan with input from marketing – for all staff and appropriate partners.
- Launch the programme with a staff roadshow.

5

PARTNER READINESS

- Identify key partners impacted by the loyalty programme.
- Discuss commercial implications of the loyalty programme and negotiate an SLA (service level agreement) if required.
- Agree on customer journey per partner and input into the BRD / SSD (see IT above).
- Work with marketing to include partners in the member engagement plan.

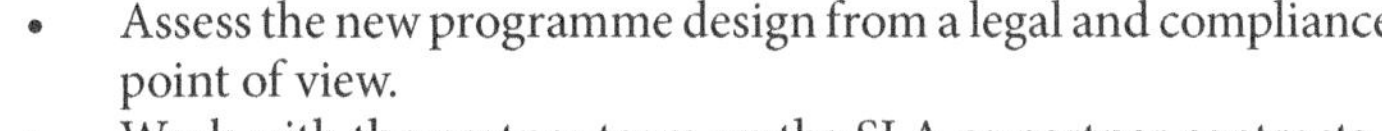

6

LEGAL & COMPLIANCE

- Assess the new programme design from a legal and compliance point of view.
- Work with the partner team on the SLA or partner contracts.
- Work with the team on Ts&Cs and the privacy policy.
- Ensure that the old to new programme migration plans meet the minimum timeframes required for member migration and any change of programme rules.
- Assess the data compliance of the chosen technical vendor or internal IT loyalty system.

7

FINANCE & ANALYTICS

- Build the commercial business case with input across the organisation.
- Confirm the commercials with partners.
- Plan the annual budgets with the loyalty team.
- Create analytical capability to provide programme performance feedback (against approved dashboards).
- Create strategic analytical capability (post go live).

Chapter 82

Challenges in implementing a loyalty programme

I find that there are a few key challenges that recur time and time again in implementing a loyalty programme that are worth highlighting to all loyalty professionals.

Let's start with defining what the strategic intent of the loyalty programme is, which we cover in chapter 17. The organisation must be aligned on the strategic question of why it is launching into loyalty. As the process will be difficult and will require a budget and change, financial and leadership commitment is vital. There will be many threats to the project and the programme launch unless the 'why' is clearly defined across the (multiple) stakeholders. We recommend that cross-functional teams are involved in this initial step, as well as those executives who are sceptical about loyalty. Address concerns and any negativity sooner rather than later in the project plan.

Secondly, how does a project team set the project timeline? It's the million dollar question and virtually impossible to answer without deeper understanding of the systems architecture. The systems critical path always dictates the project timing; staff training plans and training cycles can play an important role in the critical path. As we expressed in chapter 40, an organisation must ensure that staff are on side and excited by the programme. At a minimum, comprehensive training is required because staff buy-in is absolutely crucial.

I would also like to highlight the importance of the commercial decision-making stage of the programme. Chapters 90–92 cover the business case inputs in detail. Critically, the business case will need to prove incrementality of performance (sales, retention, or other) versus costs to run the programme plus upfront build costs (which can be depreciated over time). The trickiest part of the commercial stage is proving the input assumptions. These can often be better trusted if there has been proof of concept projects or external case studies that are relevant and impactful.

As we discussed in earlier chapters, many companies are striving for customer centricity. The loyalty programme will generate data and ultimately help with the journey to customer centricity. However, don't think that data will change the strategy. Customer centricity adds the science to the soul of a company. This shouldn't completely change strategic direction but rather enhance it. The loyalty programme is a feedback loop for the customer-centric organisation. Change management processes are required to achieve this, with top leaders being incentivised against customer KPIs, not only traditional sales performance.

> **Customer centricity is the ultimate end game; it requires change management at the top of the organisation.**

Without question, a major hurdle is the technology solution to deliver the programme. The organisation may need to build within its own IT division or bring in an external loyalty vendor. The technology decision must also take the customer service channels (website, app, WhatsApp, and the like) into account. The decision of which vendor to use will depend on the programme design, the culture match between the company and vendor, and the price. Unfortunately, too many selections are made purely on price, rather than experience and loyalty capability.

Chapter 83

Creating the right team to run the loyalty programme

Team structures will obviously vary depending on the complexity of the loyalty offering and the size of the organisation. For a simple programme, we recommend the structure below. Some loyalty organisations are operating with a headcount of 100 staff or more so the structure is merely a guideline.

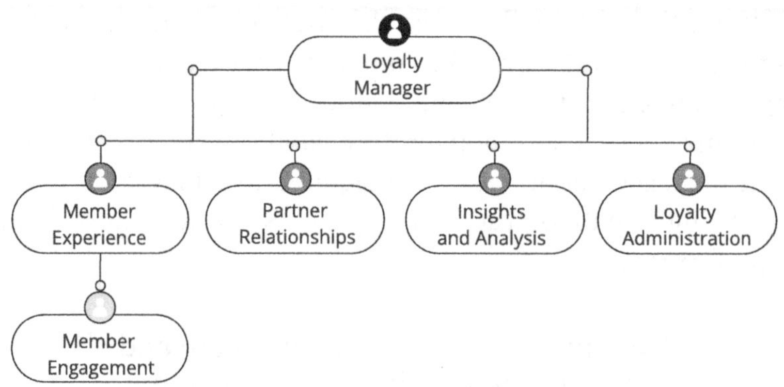

Proposed organisational structure framework

Loyalty Manager: The role of the manager should be to lead the team and ensure that all relevant stakeholders in the organisation are fully abreast of the programme's strategy and performance. The loyalty manager is also most likely to hold accountability for the budget and relationship with any external technical vendors.

Member experience & engagement: This team must keep the loyalty value proposition fresh and innovative. Create a roadmap of enhancements that will improve member benefits, drive transactional and non-transactional behaviours, and enhance the overall brand experience. This role will also manage the loyalty brand and its application across all communications. For this reason, I recommend that member engagement sits within the same team. This role will create and execute the detailed member engagement plan outlined in chapter 29. They will also work with the insights and analysis teams for pre- and post-campaign data selection and campaign results, respectively. Marketing agencies (creative, digital, CRM and media) will work most closely with this team.

Partner relationships: Should the programme have partners, this role will manage the day-to-day relationships with these partners. It will vary from strategic partner choice to contract negotiations and agreement on a required SLA (service level agreement), including setting an annual plan to ensure appropriate inclusion in the member engagement communications. The role must manage partner performance using insights gained from campaigns and partner participation in the loyalty programme.

Insights and analysis: Potentially, this portfolio could require a team of individuals. Initially, though, it could be one analyst who works diligently with the insights derived from the loyalty engine's dashboard. In my experience, this function is operationally required for campaign preparation and post campaign analysis, as well as ongoing assessment of the programme performance (against KPIs – see chapter 94). More strategically, however, this portfolio should grow to drive customer insight across the organisation. Strategic customer segmentation and AI-driven personalisation will both fall heavily within this team's portfolio.

Loyalty administration: This role will support the entire team, which does not make it any less significant. There will be customer service queries that the company's call centre may not be equipped to handle, fraud processes that require a manual intervention, and ongoing support across every touch point. Whoever fills this role is every loyalty manager's hero!

Chapter 84

Managing privacy challenges in the loyalty environment

Described as the 'perfect storm',[61] privacy challenges should be at the top of every loyalty manager's agenda. Data privacy laws have changed dramatically in most territories over the past three to five years.

Customers will typically indicate that they don't want their data to be used. However, if there is a benefit in sharing data, customers will be more willing to tick the permission box. According to *The Future of Loyalty Report 2023*, 51% of consumers are willing to let brands use purchase history to make brand experiences more relevant. However, it does depend on the type of data. The report states that consumers are least willing to share health-related information.

> **Customers think it is fair to share data if they get something valuable in return. — YouGov[62]**

Practically, the legislation has implications for every loyalty manager. In particular, the systems architecture that you use (and this is not just the external loyalty vendor) across the entire organisation must be geared to handle and understand data privacy laws. In particular, data residency and transfer legislation can create obstacles for cloud-based solutions. Ensure that your IT teams understand these regulatory requirements before implementing a cloud-based solution that may fall short of the law.

There are different layers of consent. For example, the General Data Protection Regulation (GDPR) makes a clear distinction between pseudonymised data and anonymised data and we need to understand this. "Pseudonymisation enables the personal data to become unidentifiable unless more information is available, whereas anonymisation allows the processing of personal data to irreversibly prevent re-identification."[63] Both techniques are used for the protection of individuals' personal data. The level of protection will dictate which technique is required and which level of consent must be reached before using such data.

An additional element from the GDPR is data portability. Data portability allows consumers to request access to their own personal data from a company (which has tracked both transactional and non-transactional activities, and other personal data) and use it for their own benefit. As very few individuals request this, organisations are not currently needing to fulfil such obligations, but it is something that they need to be aware of and have the capability to action should it be requested. It is becoming more prominent in the sports industry, where professional athletes require the portability of their personal data between coaches.

As companies serving their customers, the 'perfect storm' must be weathered; there is no avoiding it. It requires the right level of governance, the right training for all required staff members, and full accountability at the top of the organisation to do the right thing. The opening theme of this chapter is a consumer's willingness to share data if they can reap the benefit. A powerful loyalty proposition can help companies to weather the storm more easily.

Chapter 85

Loyalty fraud

Unfortunately, many measures are introduced into the loyalty ecosystem to prevent fraud and these in turn create friction in the loyalty experience. Loyalty fraud is a hot topic for all loyalty managers – and not a simple one to solve.

I have had the pleasure of working in a collective fraud group with many loyalty leaders in the South African industry and many points made in this chapter come from deep discussions in this group. The group is established to assist all loyalty managers to address the various pain points created by customer or staff fraud. The participants share learnings and solutions to assist each other. I highly recommend such a supportive industry approach for every market.

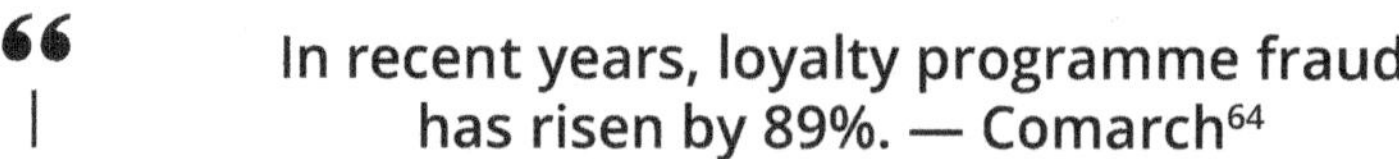

> **In recent years, loyalty programme fraud has risen by 89%. — Comarch[64]**

Without question, the number one driver of loyalty fraud is staff. I always say to programme operators that as soon as they launch, they will have fraud in the system created by their own team. This absolutely horrifies many loyalty professionals, and I am asked why we can't create a fraud-proof system. To make a programme 100% water-tight and fraud-proof from day one would require so many rules, regulations, and cross checks that the actual customer experience would be unpalatable for the majority of your customers who have no intention of defrauding you.

The most common fraudulent loyalty activities by staff include swiping a loyalty card when a non-member transacts. If a till operator who earns £500 per month is swiping grocery transactions up to £2000 per week, that's a sure sign of fraudulent staff behaviour. Triggers to track this are frequency of card swipes to earn points or benefits and time between transactions. Conversely, staff may redeem members' points. If the loyalty number of a member is remembered and used by staff on a full paying transaction, the number of points incorrectly redeemed from the unknowing customer's account can be converted into cash and pocketed by the staff member.

Customers are equally guilty, of course; we see the following activities time and time again. Returns processes struggle to handle loyalty fraud. High value items are purchased and real-time points are allocated to members' accounts then redeemed immediately. Within returns' policy timelines, the goods are returned and customers are refunded the value of goods whilst having earned and redeemed a high volume of points and benefits. Fictitious accounts for new or child members are created if there are joining bonus vouchers or child birthday rewards. Once the benefits or vouchers are redeemed, the member accounts lie dormant.

There are teams of professionals working to minimise the impact of fraud and it would be unprofessional of me to leave this chapter with no indication of how to overcome such activities. To do so would be like ripping off the plaster and leaving the wound wide open. Chapter 86 is dedicated to loyalty fraud mitigation.

Chapter 86

Loyalty fraud mitigation

Mitigating fraud deserves a book in its own right. I would like to acknowledge all founding members of the loyalty fraud group in South Africa for their openness and transparency, which has helped each brand learn from the others in creating a loyalty industry learning platform to target loyalty fraud.

In addition to loyalty professionals working together, the systems architecture's role in preventing loyalty fraud is critical. Most loyalty vendors have fraud prevention capability as part of their core offering.

> **The challenge of finding the balance between customer experience, effortless and simple loyalty, and proper security and anti-fraud measures has never been more real. — Antavo[65]**

Some of the ways to help mitigate fraud may seem very manual in a world of automation. The fraud group I refer to earlier has members of various sized organisations in the South African market. The larger corporates have forensic teams, and the smaller companies manage with just the loyalty manager managing the fraud investigations. What is clear, regardless of company size, is that fraud reporting needs to be in place and automated to pick up certain triggers or patterns that predict fraudulent or outlier behaviour. Such reports can either be created by internal company BI (business intelligence) reporting or by an external vendor, if appropriate.

One of the most powerful mitigation tools for future fraud prevention is to 'name and shame' the guilty people; this is easier with staff than customers. A disciplinary process or even criminal proceedings will harness fear among potential staff fraudsters. In addition, convey simple messages in all staff training that everything is monitored throughout the loyalty system.

For customer fraudsters, the company approach may be different. Often a warning letter asking the customer to be aware that fraudulent behaviour has been identified suffices, stating that should it continue, forensic investigation will begin. Customers most often rectify their behaviour after a warning. However, more serious cases need a heavier hand and forensic teams must lead the way. Initially, loyalty accounts will be blocked while the investigation is processed. In the case of financial fraud, financial services organisations often have sophisticated databases to measure against. If a customer has been flagged as fraudulent in the rest of the business, the same flag alert is also applied to the loyalty account. Retailers are unlikely to have this process in place in the same manner.

As prepared as you may think you are, as soon as the loyalty programme operator and its partner in loyalty technology have created a fraud-proof environment, a clever loophole will be identified either by staff or customers. Our recommendation is to work closely with your technology provider, train staff well, and take the subject of loyalty fraud very seriously, with it always top of the agenda.

Chapter 87

Loyalty technology: friend or foe?

Throughout this book, we have referred to the technology roadmap or the cost of technology. It goes without saying that deciding on the technology to drive and support the loyalty design is important and highly strategic. However, it is wildly misunderstood throughout many organisations.

Firstly, you need to decide whether to outsource the technology capability for the loyalty solution or to build it in-house. In an effort to simplify the complexity of the broader IT functionality, the following are the main components of the loyalty system.

Start with a **loyalty rules engine**. This is the heart of the loyalty solution and is described in detail in chapter 89. The loyalty rules engine must track behavioural triggers from actions and assign rewards according to programme rules. There are other critical requirements of the rules engine that cover financial governance and fraud detection capability.

Depending on the programme design and member benefits, if monetary rewards are included, a **treasury management system** is needed. This will manage the auditable process of allocating rewards and the cost of rewards to the appropriate parts of the organisation.

It also manages flows of accruals and redemptions between partners if operating a multi-partner programme.

Every member record needs to be managed and stored in a database known as the **customer data warehouse**. The database needs to track behaviours, member loyalty account status, and customer permissions. If there are multiple data sources, it is critical to achieve a single view of each customer with the single member identifier.

Customer engagement encompasses the marketing automation or campaign management tool to execute automated triggered campaigns and planned communications within the member engagement framework. How these campaigns are executed is a media decision as they affect the platform's ability to push communications via various channels (email, SMS, WhatsApp, app notifications, or gamified experiences).

Dynamic offer management is a programme's capability to generate personalised experiences and offers to members based on AI-driven decisioning. Some platforms can deliver this in real time, which is preferable.

Data insights and reporting: Loyalty platforms generate dashboards with programme and campaign performance metrics, which must deliver measurement against approved KPIs. Ideally, such capability should drive strategic data insight to aid an organisation's customer-centric strategy.

Customer channels can be built in to some loyalty platforms. However, as this isn't always the case, it needs to be addressed separately to ensure that it is not forgotten. The channel choice may require anything from website, mobisite, app, WhatsApp, or traditional USSD string communications.

Chapter 88

The technology decision – managing the RFP process

Many organisations decide to outsource the technical capability for their loyalty programme. From our experience, there are three types of organisation which are likely to respond to an issued RFP (request for proposal). Firstly, there are specialised loyalty technical partners with pre-built loyalty technology that might need slight customisation to meet requirements. Secondly, digital or CRM agencies that may have built a loyalty platform for clients previously but this isn't their core offering. Thirdly, large IT consulting firms also offer such services but typically respond to an RFP with a customised build.

Our recommendation is to focus on the pre-built martech providers who build and manage loyalty technology as their core focus. There are two main technology research services that can assist in evaluating the martech landscape, namely Gartner (*Gartner's Market Guide for Loyalty Management*) and Forrester (*Forrester's Wave around Loyalty Program Technologies*). However, we find that some vendors that are not listed in either report have superb loyalty capability and should be considered. Therefore, also ensure that potentially smaller, local vendors are evaluated as part of this process.

Who should be part of the RFP evaluation team? We highly recommend a cross-functional approach to ensure all internal stakeholders are engaged and part of the selection process. Typically, evaluation teams will include executives from IT, marketing, finance, and procurement, as well as loyalty or CRM specialists and, sometimes, HR. The external loyalty consultant asks the very difficult questions on behalf of the loyalty team and needs to have sufficient experience to know where typical pain points lie.

It goes without saying that the RFP must evaluate the technology functionality. In particular, focus on ensuring that this functionality can respond to the bespoke loyalty programme design in question. There are too many subpoints to list here in one single chapter to cover all functionality options. However, from my experience, the capability of a vendor under review is most often the easiest to evaluate and simplest to compare against other vendors.

Over and above the technology's main loyalty functionality, the data management and security, and its ability to respond to data privacy legislation are critical (see chapter 84). I suggest that RFP teams probe deeply into the vendor's fraud detection capability, the reporting and dashboard functionality, and the product development cycles. The loyalty team needs to be sure that the vendor will release fresh innovation and technology improvements over the period of engagement.

Obviously, price will play a significant part in the RFP team's decision but my recommendation is that it should not be the most weighted decision point. Consider also the upfront build costs and integrations, as well as ongoing license fees.

> **Do we have a cultural fit with the chosen technical partner, and can we work well together — especially if things go wrong?**

And finally, the RFP team must evaluate the team who will be managing the account and the cultural fit of the vendor as they will be significant partners in the loyalty project.

Chapter 89

What exactly is a loyalty rules engine?

I have asked Charles Ehredt, CEO Currency Alliance, to be the sole contributor to this chapter as he is in a league of his own and understands how best to share loyalty technical knowledge.

❝ —— Contribution by Charles Ehredt

The loyalty rules engine is probably the most powerful yet under-appreciated module (or tool) in a loyalty marketing stack of software.

The loyalty rules engine enables fine-tuning incentives for various customer segments so you don't give away too many points for routine behaviours, but then can offer very attractive incentives to get customers to perform actions or make purchases that grow the value of your business. These could include birthday bonuses, encouraging more shopping during your off-peak hours, or double points on distressed inventory.

When companies are designing a new loyalty programme, the first thing they should do is make a long list of all the behaviours they would like customers to perform. The list needs to be longer than 'Buy more stuff'. The idea here is that most businesses probably want to influence 20–40 specific behaviours that lead either to increased sales or greater lifetime value (LTV).

The desire or priority to sell specific products or services changes over time, so points-based incentives can be used to create more urgency or motivation among customers if optimised for the specific context of a potential sale.

There are three types of context for a transaction that the rules engine ideally needs to consider:

- The characteristics of the customer (frequency/recency/LTV).
- The characteristics of the product or service (margin or perishability, etc.).
- The situation in which the transaction takes place.

The point here is that the 'context' of nearly every customer touchpoint is different and it makes little sense to always offer exactly the same incentive (i.e. 1% in points).

The customer's context typically includes shopping behaviour, purchase history, tier status, demographic data, and psychographic insights. The loyalty rules engine should have access to such insight in order to dynamically adapt the incentive to increase conversion.

The context for product or service includes the availability of the inventory, its availability at a specific time, the profit margin, and any associated opportunity cost. The context of the situation includes all other factors that can influence the customer's predisposition to take an action at a specific time – such as the weather, the time of day, the day of the month, and how convenient it is for the customer to engage via a specific channel or visit a specific store.

Loyalty rules can be set to respond to all such triggers in order to maximise the probability of driving a specific customer action. Such personalisation has remained elusive in most loyalty programmes but with the right loyalty rules engine or combination of rules engines, it's not difficult to tailor engagement in this way.

——————————— ”

Chapter 90

How to calculate loyalty programme uplift

In chapter 25, we suggest that the business case of a loyalty programme is assessed as the seventh step in the nine-step process to a loyalty programme launch. Virtually every single discussion with loyalty brand executives starts with, "How much will this project cost?" And unfortunately, I never have the magic wand to conjure up an immediate response. There are so many critical components to creating a robust business case.

The next two chapters separate the upfront expenses, which often can be depreciated over time (these are often referred to as capex – capital expenditure), and the ongoing expenses of running the programme (often referred to as opex – operating expenses). The expense lines of the business case are somewhat easier to predict than the commercial uplift expected from a loyalty programme. This chapter outlines the approach to understanding the income drivers of a loyalty programme. Obviously, the structure of the programme (see chapter 20), the benefits and rewards design, as well as the programme rules, all play a part in the cost and the income drivers.

First and foremost, the main focus for income in loyalty programmes is incremental sales. In chapter 17, we propose a 4–6% increase in sales performance as a tried and tested input for all loyalty business cases. Some loyalty professionals work with a 10% incrementality but I prefer a more conservative approach. How does a company reach the magic 4–6%? I suggest two approaches. One is a top down approach, whereby 4–6% is applied to current revenue performance (plus inflation and planned revenue increases, like new store openings or product launches). Simultaneously, the commercial case needs to calculate a bottom-up review applying loyalty principles. These calculations need to take into account estimated volume of programme members, activity rates, current spend, transaction frequency, and basket or transaction size. If previous proof of concept campaigns or loyalty initiatives have been delivered in the business, the output data from these should be used. Once the incremental revenue calculations are complete, we recommend that the business also reviews the margin impact of the programme uplift. If the gross margin of the business is stated at 40%, then we recommend a 40% calculation of incremental sales as a more accurate indicator of programme uplift.

> **The more accurate review of income from the loyalty programme is incremental gross margin rather than sales.**

If a programme design has partners, there are income drivers from the partnership relationships. Partners may be required to pay a fee to be part of the loyalty programme. There may be the opportunity to sell a points currency at a marginally higher rate per point than the rate for which it gets redeemed. Bank interest gained from partners' payment for issued points (before they are redeemed by members) should also be included.

Data is a currency. If a programme is operating with partners and merchants, sales of aggregated customer data can also be attributed to loyalty programme income drivers.

Finally, if the programme is a subscription-based offering, then, clearly, members will pay monthly or annual fees, which creates an income line for the loyalty business case. Careful consideration needs to be given to attrition of member volumes before this income line is guaranteed.

Chapter 91

The cost of building a loyalty programme (capex)

The cost of the programme build obviously depends on many factors and, in particular, the decision regarding in-house IT solution or external technical vendor. Either way, the IT cost and other capitalised expenses need to be accounted for. The number of years a business will depreciate its cost varies and needs to be assessed by the senior financial team.

In a simplified approach to the business case costs, there are three main areas of capitalised expenditure to build a loyalty programme: systems, people, and marketing.

Firstly, the upfront systems costs should cover the loyalty engine and all its component parts, which we introduced in chapter 87. If this is an in-house solution, the robust set of questions (set out in chapter 88) needs to be asked of the in-house IT team to ensure that all requirements (like the database, data security, and hosting rules) are met. It is extremely unlikely that the cost quoted by an external vendor at RFP stage will be the final allocated cost. Most projects require the detailed systems specifications to be defined, against which an accurate project timeline and build cost can be calculated. Remember to include the cost of required integrations into programme partners, customer facing channels, or enterprise systems (like point of sale and financial systems). Often a middleware solution can simplify the complexity of multiple integrations. If this is the case, this has an associated cost for the project. Finally, customer-facing channels, such as app, website, or communication channels (like WhatsApp) will all require development to ensure a seamless member experience. Some external vendors include these costs; others do not.

Secondly, preparing staff for a loyalty programme launch is high on the agenda and we have repeatedly emphasised the importance of ensuring the loyalty brand's personnel are on-side and motivated to support the programme. For the cost calculation, we also recommend that all external consultants are charged to capex. In addition, all training costs (time, trainers, and materials), which may include additional costs from an external systems vendor, should also be capitalised in the business case.

Teams often debate whether to allocate the cost of launch marketing to the upfront costs. There are significant upfront design costs like the loyalty programme logo and brand identity, all marketing communication collateral, and customer-facing channels, such as website and app. Some companies launch their loyalty programme with investment into above-the-line launches using traditional media like TV, radio, and, of course, digital channels.

> **Big bang programme launches in traditional media channels are costly but can boost initial member sign up rates at launch.**

Again, this can be a capitalised expense as it is a once-off launch cost. In addition, if the strategy requires old programme members to be migrated to the new programme, there undoubtedly will be associated marketing costs. Such costs will vary according to communication strategy and any incentives offered to entice existing members to engage with the new programme.

Chapter 92

Business as usual – the cost of running a loyalty programme

The commercial evaluation of a loyalty programme is likely to be reviewed over a number of years. This is recommended, as taking a one-year view is unlikely to yield positive results. As we have stated throughout this book, loyalty is not a campaign but a long-term strategic approach. Such a strategy will require time to create a positive return on investment. We recommend that commercial modelling should address the capex costs outlined in the previous chapter plus three years of operating costs. Using such a formula also allows accurate assessment of external vendor costs so that the weighting of implementation costs versus ongoing license fees can be evened out over the three-year period.

> **For ongoing programme costs, we must place greater emphasis on regular member engagement.**

Once again, for simplicity, we can allocate ongoing costs as follows: systems, people, marketing, and customer rewards (i.e. programme benefits).

Systems costs must cover any external vendor license fees, which may be structured as a flat monthly fee, a per member cost, a per transaction cost, or any combination of associated costs. It is critical to understand such costs, especially if there are formulae to include per transaction costs. If an in-house or external system integrates with any other piece of IT architecture, there are always potential running costs. A simple voucher redemption may incur a per voucher fee. There will be hosting costs and potential data warehouse or security fees. The cost of executing campaigns may be included in a vendor's licence fee, but the media channels through which communications are sent will incur additional cost.

Marketing teams may work with agencies to deliver the primary focus of the member engagement plan and ongoing programme awareness campaigns. Ensure agency fees are included to cover all elements of the loyalty operational communications (outlined in chapter 32) and all other communications to drive programme KPIs. If the loyalty programme uses physical cards as well as digital channels, there are hard costs for design, print, production, and distribution of these physical cards.

Running a loyalty programme requires resources. Some companies outsource all elements of the programme to external agencies that take responsibility for all elements of executing a great loyalty experience for programme members. More often than not, however, the programme will be managed in-house, and chapter 83 offers an initial insight into an organisational structure to run the loyalty programme. For either situation, full costs must be allocated to the programme budget. To improve the programme, some organisations augment loyalty expertise with consultants, introducing world-class thinking and innovation. These costs must also be allocated to the budget.

Finally, there is the cost of the entire customer experience for members. Programme rewards like points and redemptions, member-only discounts, member-only experiences, and surprise-and-delight tactics must all be allocated as a cost in the annual budget. Forgive me if this is a statement of the obvious, but rewards must be correlated to the input data in the business case so programme performance is directly aligned to associated costs.

Chapter 93

The value of a point

Why is calculating the value of a point such a difficult process? It is most definitely getting easier as loyalty brands simplify their programmes and introduce more educational communications to ensure members truly understand the value they are getting back from the programme. Many programmes clearly communicate the value of a point for the redemption exchange, but others are still less transparent about the real value when calculated against the earn activities.

All credit to the loyalty brands that clearly state the redemption exchange rate, for example 10 points = $1, and re-iterate the members' points balance and monetary equivalent on every communication and at every touch point. However, how many programmes explain the whole loyalty programme economics clearly enough? Let's take three beauty retailers to illustrate the customer experience of calculating their real reward value.

Brand	Communicated earn rate	Communicated redemption value	Calculated % as value back on spend	Value of 1 point
Sorbet (variable redemption rate per tier)	1 point for every R1 spent (South African currency: ZAR) - same across all tiers	3000 points = R50 3000 points = R100 3000 points = R150 3000 points = R200	Tier 1: 1.7% Tier 2: 3.3% Tier 3: 5% Tier 4: 6.7%	Tier 1: R0.017 Tier 2: R0.033 Tier 3: R0.050 Tier 4: R0.067
Sephora	1 point for every $1 spent	500 points = $10 off	2%	$0,020
Ulta Beauty (variable earn rate per tier)	1 point for every $1 spent 1 point for every $1.25 spent 1 point for every $1.5 spent	100 points = $3 500 points = $17.50 2000 points = $125	Tier 1: 3.0%-6.3% Tier 2: 3.8%-7.8% Tier 3: 4.5%-9.4%	Tier 1: $0.030 Tier 2: $0.035 Tier 3: $0.063

Beauty industry - points value calculation

The value of one point becomes an almost meaningless number as it can't be compared across different brands. The calculated percentage back to members is a more accurate unit for comparison. The table shows the complexity of tiering and how carefully members need to evaluate the rewards value of a programme. For example, Sephora Beauty Insider comprises three types of programme benefits (see chapter 72) and value back to members. Its 'savings' proposition is only one third of the programme's full offering and therefore assessing a 2% value back on spend isn't a fair representation of customer value from Sephora's Beauty Insider programme.

In chapter 90, we consider the commercial drivers of a loyalty programme and how a multi-partner programme can buy and sell its loyalty currency with partners, at different rates for the earn and the redemption transaction. Each transaction offers the opportunity for the programme operator to make a marginal profit per point.

> **"A large coalition loyalty programme can sell hundreds of billions of points each year, making those fraction of a cent profits quickly add up.**
> **— Loyalty & Reward Co[66]**

Some industries are more likely to use variable rates for points or miles than others. An airline frequent flyer programme is very likely to have different redemption rates for flight redemptions versus non-flight redemptions. It will also have different earn rates for flights across different cabins or for members in different tiers. The earn rate of a mile will differ if earned through a co-branded bank-airline payment card. In a nutshell, I refer back to chapter 27 where we encourage simplicity for members. There is a dark science behind the value of points which many companies wish to continue in order to mask the real value. I believe today's customer is way too smart to succumb to the dark science for much longer.

Chapter 94

Programme KPIs – loyalty managers' daily mantra

No matter what Key Performance Indicators (KPIs) are recommended in a chapter like this, every reader is likely to approach their own list of KPIs differently. The recommended set of KPIs will depend on so many variables, like programme structure, company priorities, industry sector, and the like. I will share what I believe is a solid starting point for loyalty managers to review and adapt.

Total members: all programmes will track membership volumes. The **acquisition rate of members** by channel and by period of time is also an important metric to assess how some activities are yielding better member sign-up rates than others.

Activity rates must be tracked. A new programme is likely to have a high activity rate as new members join and transact; they may or may not remain active. Over time, many programmes settle at 50% activity rate, but 60–70% activity is a better target. It is debatable how to measure activity per industry, over what period of time? In our opinion, this needs to be assessed against **average member frequency** statistics.

Time to activate after enrolment becomes a very powerful indicator of how a member will engage with the loyalty brand in the future. This will vary vastly per industry but should be measured over time to avoid a slowdown in activation rates.

Incremental sales is a critical KPI, as we explain in chapter 90. We recommend 4–6% increase in sales, over and above inflation and like-for-like sales growth. Some loyalty professionals refer to 10% incrementality as a target. We prefer a more conservative approach. True measurement of value back to the company is applying a gross margin calculation to measure **incremental gross margin contribution** from the programme.

Within the revenue calculation, **member frequency, transaction size, number of products held,** and **average customer value** will be measured. Comparing such performance with non-members, however, can be meaningless due to member self-selection, which we have introduced earlier in this book.

Tenure and **churn** are two measures that will maintain focus on member retention. Tenure is often a trigger to celebrate with members as they reach significant milestones. We estimate that a loyalty programme can aid in reducing churn by approximately 10% in year one.

Redemption performance is critical to measure. A healthy loyalty programme will see higher redemption rates. Average performance sits at 50% of points redeemed but strong and established programmes will reach 80% or more.

Loyalty penetration of total sales is also a critical measure. In the retail industry we recommend 65–70% as a good result, but I am delighted to see so many companies now reporting more than 80% of sales through loyalty member sales.

Customer lifetime value is undoubtedly one of the key indicators to measure, but it is widely misunderstood. In its most simple format, it measures customer value over a customer's lifespan with the brand.

ROI isn't always included in programme KPIs but rather used as a business case review indicator. Many loyalty professionals consider 200% to be a strong ROI result.

Chapter 95

Loyalty programme liability: friend or foe?

There is simply no better expert in the loyalty world than Len Llaguno to answer this question. Len has generously contributed this whole chapter from his deep experience in running KYROS, the only actuarial firm globally that is solely focused on many of the world's greatest loyalty programmes.

“ —— Contribution by Len Llaguno

What is loyalty liability? It's a balance sheet liability representing the expected cost of points currently outstanding (i.e. issued but not yet redeemed or expired). There are some accounting nuances that complicate things, but this definition is probably sufficient for most loyalty marketers.

Why is it so important? For your colleagues in finance and accounting, the liability is important because there are regulations that require accurate financial reporting of the liability. For loyalty marketers, the liability itself is less important. Instead, it's the understanding of redemption costs that comes from the liability analysis that is critical.

Why? Because redemption cost is the single largest expense in a loyalty programme business model. If you care about the health of your business model, you should care deeply about accurately estimating redemption cost.

Redemption costs differ from typical business expenses because they are uncertain. That is, quantifying the redemption cost of points issued today requires an estimate of how many of these points will eventually get redeemed. We see that most programmes have bad redemption cost estimates, ranging from underestimating by tens of millions of dollars to overshooting by 50%. Very rarely do we see it accurately stated without proper actuarial techniques. For some loyalty marketers, this could mean they are running their business into the ground and they don't even know it.

Liability management best practice is critical. First, ensure that you have a sound actuarial estimate for your redemption costs. Second, don't focus on the liability. Focus on the cost/benefit trade-off. It can be neatly summarised in this formula:

> **Expected Future Profit =**
> **[Expected Future Spend] x**
> **(1 - COGS% - Redemption Cost %)**
> **— Len Llaguno**

Expected Future Profit (or EFP) represents the expected profit that a member will generate in the future. It's comprised of a volume component (Expected Future Spend) and a margin component (1 – COGS% [cost of goods sold %] – Redemption Cost %). This formula makes clear what a loyalty programme is trying to do – i.e. sacrificing some margin (giving away some redemption cost %) in the hope of getting more volume (increasing expected future spend) in such a way that drives an increase to EFP.

If you have an understanding of this cost/benefit trade off, it's much easier to put the liability into context. This helps convert finance counterparts from loyalty skeptics to loyalty advocates.

Section 5

Concluding thoughts

Chapter 96

Emotional loyalty

There is no question that brands wish to create an emotional connection with their customers. An emotional relationship will last longer and be more fulfilling than a purely rational relationship based on transactional experiences only. Most customers, however, think that they are rational but tend to behave in more emotional ways. This sentiment is supported by the insights from IAG Loyalty in *Getting to the point of loyalty in a cost-of-living crisis – 2022*. IAG Loyalty states that "When redeeming, 80% of people consider themselves rational decision makers and 20% emotional decision makers … Ultimately, people collect points rationally in order to spend them on emotional purchases." The report continues to state that "we go on holiday to make fun, not to make sense," which entirely supports how travel is a hugely emotional part of loyalty programmes. For that reason, we see that so many retail banking programmes specialise in travel as a primary redemption choice. Banking is rational; travel is more likely to be emotional.

Emotional loyalty isn't created by a single action; it is the result of successful strategies and plans coming together to better serve the customer. Each chapter in this book is dedicated to one of the component parts. A company cannot execute on a single plan to drive emotional loyalty; it is rather an output of a carefully curated and superbly executed loyalty strategy. Customers will experience a greater emotional connection to a brand if they trust the brand. Loyalty clearly plays its role in building trust through personalisation and seamless experiences. Outlined in chapters 50 and 51, we highlight 'by invitation only' and 'surprise and delight' as benefits which we believe drive an emotional response.

> **Emotional connection translates into a better share of consumer spending with customers typically spending twice as much with brands that they are loyal to and having a 300% lifetime value. — Motista[67]**

Brands that build a sense of community and togetherness will drive a greater sense of emotional connection. Loyalty brands' ability to use their programme for sustainability and environmental causes, as well as harnessing the collective effort of members to aid a higher purpose, are documented in chapters 60 and 61. Harley Davidson has been a brand that generates a sense of community through its Harley Owners Club. It has just launched the H-D membership, which "gives the community of riders and non-riders a new way to connect … and to really make their experience with the brand as personalised as possible," according to Jochen Zeitz, Chairman, President, and CEO, Harley-Davidson. What H-D membership is trying to achieve takes emotional loyalty to another level.

Ultimately, the real test of the strength of a customer's emotional loyalty to a brand happens when things go wrong. Does the customer feel enough positive connection to forgive the brand that has just failed them, with or without a loyalty programme? As we said is chapter 5, loyalty is just the icing on the cake; it is not the entire brand experience. The role loyalty plays takes place before any brand failure and it works to build trust through personalised connections and experiences.

Chapter 97

Advocacy – the ultimate loyalty

The ultimate loyalty is (of course) when customers speak positively about their favourite brand. In chapter 7, we discussed how for many years the Net Promoter Score has been an industry measure for overall customer experience based on the single question of "How likely are you to recommend this product or company?" According to Bain & Company (the owners of the NPS methodology), "Bain analysis shows that sustained value creators – companies that achieve long-term profitable growth – have NPS two times higher than the average company."

Throughout this book we have suggested different ways for brands to engage with their members and, in some cases, reward them for their participation in activities like refer a friend and social media engagement. One could argue that neither are real advocacy as the activities are incentivised. Another channel of paid-for influence is via social media influencers. According to InMoment's *2022 Experience Trends Report*,[68] 50% of consumers had used influencer codes in the past six months or less. There is no question that rewarded or paid-for influencer strategies may have a positive sales effect, but true brand loyalty will be achieved through a well-executed brand and loyalty strategy.

In a world of cookie-less digital marketing and changing customer perceptions towards targeted brand advertising, referral programmes may have just found their place. In a more formal loyalty programme structure, referral programmes can certainly unlock value for the loyalty brand. According to Forrester, the following four benefits can be achieved against a well-executed referral programme: 1. high-value customer leads; 2. incremental sales and revenue; 3. lower cost per acquisition; and 4. increased customer engagement.[69] This is supported by The Harvard Business Review, which states: "We studied 10,000 accounts in a large German bank over a period of three years and found that customers obtained through referrals are both more loyal and more valuable than other customers."[70]

> **Loyalty done right should naturally create a ripple effect. Happy customers tell others, rippling the brand affinity across their network.**
> **— Erin Raese, SVP Revenue Annex Cloud[71]**

Utopia, however, has to be the natural ripple effect of real brand advocates rather than paid-for referrals through a structured or less formal incentivised programme. In chapter 96, we described the emotional connection brands can make with customers if they get all elements of the customer experience right. Loyalty plays its role and is the icing on the top of the cake. It is that feeling when the customer is prepared to forgive a brand when things go wrong no matter what. These customers are most likely to create a bigger ripple effect than paid-for referral programmes.

Long live emotional loyalty! Long live advocacy!

Chapter 98

Why we are obsessed with retention

There is not a loyalty professional in the world who does not obsess over retention. It is high on every loyalty team's KPIs (see chapter 94). There are age-old quotes about how much less it costs an organisation to keep a customer than to acquire new customers. In chapter 31, we highlight that retention and penetration are two outcomes of loyalty more significant than acquisition and cost efficiencies (outlined in the REAP model). Some industries, like fitness clubs and subscription renewals (for example telco or insurances), are faced with more aggressive customer churn than others. This chapter will share some global best practice from brands that are creating engaging platforms to beat churn.

> **A loyalty programme is more than just a retention programme so let's start exploring how to unlock loyalty's full potential as an asset value creation.**

Virgin Active is a global household name for fitness clubs. Worldwide, this industry battles with large volumes of lapsing customers after the initial rush of new year enthusiasm. Virgin Active has just launched its Virgin Active Rewards programme. Its main purpose seems to be to drive regular engagement and community. Members are rewarded across various challenges, like consistency of workouts, consistency of reaching weekly goals – both rewarded against streaks, and tier points for engaging in non-transactional activities. Higher tiers unlock deeper discounts at partners.

Discovery Vitality has created a platform to drive constant engagement, which is outlined in chapter 79. Loyalty professionals like to use the term 'stickiness'; in Vitality's case, stickiness is achieved through frequency of engagement combined with long-term incentives. There are weekly engagement activities and weekly rewards. Greater rewards are achieved through more significant, longer term goals like improved health and financial wellness scores.

Bilt and Genesis are two brands worth highlighting for their differentiated approach to address churn, both from unlikely industries to be commended for innovation. Bilt Rewards, as part of its rental payment platform, is the first global programme to reward tenants for better rental behaviours thus reducing churn for landlords. It not only motivates tenants, but also creates a solution for landlords. In addition, positive rental behaviours improve credit bureau ratings for home buyers and therefore enable improved interest rates on home loans. Power Shout, the reward offering from Genesis, a New Zealand-based energy company, offers free hours of power with flexibility of use. It encourages app engagement for tips on energy management. Genesis attributes 11% reduction in churn to Power Shout and, interestingly, state that 23% of new customers say Power Shout is one of the reasons for joining.[72]

Rory Sutherland is no stranger to the loyalty and marketing industry. He is Vice Chairman of advertising giant Ogilvy. He illustrates that simple tactics of highlighting to a member how long they have been with a brand can create enormous recognition. Amex places the words 'member since 21' on its prestigious American Express card to create that sense of tenure. British Airways offers lifetime tier points that actually yield no material benefit other than a feeling of recognition.

Chapter 99

Consumer psychology in loyalty: we are human, after all

If there is one professional to whom our loyalty industry turns for insight about how consumer psychology impacts loyalty performance, it's Yuping Liu-Thompkins. Yuping is Director of The Loyalty Science Lab, Strome College of Business, at Old Dominion University and we are partners in the Customer Strategy Network.[73]

Let's start with the power of loyalty to respond to a human's basic need to belong. If the brand's loyalty programme really excels in creating a personalised brand experience, it will build trust with customers and ultimately help customers feel like they belong.

So many of the insights shared in this chapter are from various interviews I have heard with Yuping on *Let's Talk Loyalty*[74] and from her articles, which can be found on www.medium.com.

> **When brands make their customers feel like they belong on their team (or in their tribe), they open up new opportunities for building lasting loyalty and increasing value.**
> **— Loyalty & Rewards Co[75]**

What I enjoy the most about the psychological insight from Yuping, is how practical its application can be in programme performance.

For example, the closer members get to a reward, how do they behave differently? It depends. Typically, if the members are just starting out with the programme, they need reassurance that they can easily make progress and that it is all worth the effort. If members are closing in on a reward or tier status upgrade, the programme should show members the progress they have made. As loyalty professionals, we can easily see how important this is in terms of how to communicate a simple monthly statement. It should not be the same for all members. The further a member is from the desired target, the more rational and practical the communication style needs to be, helping the member understand step by step how to reach the next tier, for example. The closer a member gets to a target, the more the communication needs to take on an emotional tone to drive excitement about how attainable the reward is.

Yuping describes how stamp cards for a coffee shop or car wash can drive accelerated frequency by using simple tactics that encourage customers to behave differently. Take, for example, a 'buy 8, get 1 free' offer. Group one will have a stamp card with eight free stamps to be filled. Group two will have ten stamps, with two pre-filled and eight free stamps to be filled. Group two will have a faster frequency cycle than group one because of the two pre-filled stamps. As consumers, we are already motivated to be closer to the end target. In fact, in both scenarios, consumers decrease time between visits as they fill the card, i.e. frequency increases.

In a separate study, Yuping delves into monetary versus non-monetary rewards (i.e. softer benefits). She advises that programme operators should also communicate the softer rewards rather than only the monetary rewards. The monetary rewards generate immediate emotion but non-monetary rewards generate a higher intensity of emotion, which creates a longer-term relationship between brand and customer.

This chapter could continue for pages and pages. It is a fascinating insight into customer loyalty because, after all, we are all human.

Chapter 100

100 favourite loyalty programmes

What better way to review the world's favourite loyalty programmes than to ask loyalty leaders from around the world. This list is composed from the responses of show guests on the renowned *Let's Talk Loyalty* podcast. Since January 2022, Paula Thomas and her co-show hosts ask all loyalty guests, "What is your favourite loyalty programme?" Guest responses are listed below in priority of number of mentions and alphabetically if in in equal position for number of mentions. The research ran until 13th July 2023.

★★★★★★★★ Starbucks Rewards
★★★★★★★ Amazon Prime
★★★★★★ Emirates Skywards
★★★★★ Qantas - Frequent Flyer
★★★★★ Sephora Beauty Insider
★★★★ Adidas adiClub
★★★★ Air Canada Aeroplan
★★★★ American Express Membership Rewards
★★★★ British Airways Executive Club
★★★★ Delta SkyMiles
★★ Boots Advantage Card
★★ Planet BrewDog
★★ Chipotle Rewards
★★ Clicks ClubCard
★★ Costa Club
★★ Duolingo
★★ Hotels.com Rewards
★★ Marriott Bonvoy
★★ MyMcDonald's Rewards
★★ Singapore Airlines KrisFlyer
★★ Starwood Preferred Guest (SPG)
★★ Tesco Clubcard
★★ United Airlines MileagePlus Rewards

Let's Talk

★The below loyalty brands are mentioned once as 'favourite programme' by loyalty leaders:

Accor Live Limitless
Air France / KLM Flying Blue
Air New Zealand Airpoints
Alaska Airlines Mileage Plan
Albert Heign Bonus
Amazon Smile
Apple Card
Baker's Delight Dough Getter
Brave Browser Brave Rewards
British Midland / BMI Diamond Club
BT Friends & Family International
Burnt Bbq & Tacos
Carrefour MyCLUB
Chewy Pack
CitiBank Citi Rewards
Clinique Smart Rewards
CommBank Awards
CommBank Yello
Co-op Membership Rewards
Crown Rewards
Deliveroo Plus
Discovery Bank Vitality Money Rewards
Discovery Health Vitality Active Rewards
DoorDash DashPass
DSW VIP
Dunkin' Rewards
Etihad Guest
GEMS Rewards Programme
Grab SG GrabRewards
H&M Membership
Harley Davidson Harley Owners Group
HDFC Bank Infinia card
Hippie Cowgirl Couture
Holiday Inn IHG® One Rewards
Humble coffee card
IBL wiiv Rewards
Jumbo Extra's
Just Eat StampCards
Kajabi
Kauai App
KFC Rewards Arcade
Kohl's Rewards
League of Legends Rewards
Lidl Plus
Marks & Spencer Sparks
Microsoft Rewards
Nike Membership
Nordstrom The Nordy Club
Old Navy Navyist Rewards
Ole & Steen App
Payback
PC Optimum
Pets at Home VIP
Porsche Club
Qantas American Express Ultimate Card
Qatar Airways Privilege Club
REI Co-op Membership
S&H Green Stamps
SAQ Inspire
Scandinavian Airlines EuroBonus
Sculpted By Aimee Sculpted Rewards
Share Rewards
ShopBack
Star Alliance
Supercheap Auto Club
SuperValu Real Rewards
Taco Bell Rewards
Taj Hotels NeuPass Programme
The Dark Star Brewery
T-Mobile Tuesdays
Uber Rewards
Ulta Beauty Ultamate Rewards
Vida e Caffè App
Virgin Red
Vodafone VeryMe Rewards
Woolworths Everyday Rewards
World of Hyatt

Chapter 101

My definition of blind loyalty

I have my husband Theo to thank for the title of this book and the name of The Blind Loyalty Trust. Both ideas were formulated during the intense and terrifying illness that caused temporary blindness in my right eye. Good things come from bad.

Blind loyalty, as defined in various dictionaries, has negative connotations like loyalty despite knowing better, implying some level of idiocy.

Potentially – and controversially – I prefer to think of blind loyalty as that absolute level of loyalty over and above the emotional loyalty and advocacy we introduced in chapters 96 and 97.

I will express my blind loyalty to two individuals who go above and beyond, standing by me throughout my illness in their professional capacity, as an illustration of my definition of blind loyalty.

Firstly, the dedicated eye surgeon who wishes to remain anonymous; he has helped me for the past 18 months. He saw me almost daily for the initial, intense three-month period, conducted three eye surgeries, giving up a family holiday for one of these emergency corneal transplants, all of which were done together with an incredible team at the hospital and his doctor's rooms, showing humility and leadership. I don't think I have ever met a professional who is so talented in his field and yet so caring to the people around him – both patients and his own team. I could not have walked this health journey with any other team. So, what is my point? No loyalty programme on earth would shift my loyalty from Dr A. Does that mean I am undermining everything mentioned in the previous chapters of this book? Not at all; some things in life are simply not contained in the definitions of a marketing profession.

The second individual I'd like to recognise for blind loyalty is the financial advisor who handled my insurance requirements at the time of illness and recuperation. He had virtually no contracts in place with our family and yet pulled out every single stop in his professional network to make sure I was able to access the benefits due for either medical or loss of income insurance. Mr B., you know who you are with your magic formula of serving your clients well despite their actual portfolio size. You have my family's loyalty for the next few generations. The products you recommend drive their own loyalty programme strategies (which I enjoy) but, as I say above, the loyalty to you is an emotional connection built on human truths.

To end, I started researching additional inspiration for this book when I was in the depths of my recent illness and I came across this quote:

> **A loyalty programme is corrective eye surgery for business. — Rory Sutherland, Vice Chairman Ogilvy**

It smacked me right between the eyes – excuse the pun. I was literally breathless because of its absolute relevance for the loyalty story I wished to express in *Blind Loyalty* and for the timing of my own corrective-eye surgery (or rather eye-saving surgery). Rory, you may never know this but your quotation had a more profound impact than you could have ever imagined.

References

Reference Number	Chapter	
1.	2	Truth and BrandMapp Loyalty Whitepaper 2022: https://truth.co.za/articles/whitepapers/
2.	2	What the British want from Loyalty Programmes 3.0 by Mando-Connect 2022: https://www.mando-connect.co.uk/what-the-british-want-from-loyalty-programmes-3/
3.	2	The Bond Brand Loyalty Report 2021: https://info.bondbrandloyalty.com/loyaltyreport-2021
4.	2	Global Loyalty Now a $323B Investment. But is it Shaping Customer Behavior? 27 June 2019: https://www.mytotalretail.com/article/global-loyalty-now-a-323b-investment-but-is-it-shaping-customer-behavior/
5.	2	On Point Loyalty Report 2020: https://onpointloyalty.com/wp-content/uploads/2020/02/On-Point-Loyalty-Top-100-Most-Valuable-Airline-Loyalty-Programs-2020.pdf
6.	6	https://www.sciencedirect.com/topics/computer-science/customer-relationship-management-system
7.	7	100 Of The Most Customer-Centric Companies 30 June 2019: https://www.forbes.com/sites/blakemorgan/2019/06/30/100-of-the-most-customer-centric-companies/
8.	7	Major honors for everest Bite Club at the International Loyalty Awards 2022: https://cibum.gr/nea/epixeiriseis/simantikes-diakriseis-gia-to-everest-bite-club-sta-international-loyalty-awards-2022/
9.	8	The Top 100 Most Customer-Centric Companies Of 2022: https://www.forbes.com/sites/blakemorgan/2022/05/01/the-top-100-most-customer-centric-companies-of-2022/?sh=4cbe7c422b38
10.	10	There are 6 challenges every data-driven marketer faces. Here's how to manage them 23 April 2019: https://martech.org/here-are-6-challenges-every-data-driven-marketers-faces-and-how-to-manage-them/
11.	12	5 keys to creating value with first-party data April 2021: https://www.thinkwithgoogle.com/intl/en-ssa/future-of-marketing/digital-transformation/sustainable-first-party-data-strategy/
12.	12	Truth and BrandMapp Loyalty Whitepaper 2019/2020: https://truth.co.za/articles/whitepapers/
13.	14	Let's Talk Loyalty #299 Dr Shorful Islam, CEO Be Data Solutions 9 November 2022: https://letstalkloyalty.com/299/
14.	14	Use Analytics And Insights To Accelerate Your Customer Experience Strategy February 2021: https://mapp.com/wp-content/uploads/2021/04/Customer-Experience-Strategy-Study-2021.pdf
15.	14	Real-Time Analytics: The Key to Unlocking Customer Insights & Driving the Customer Experience: https://www.sas.com/en_ph/whitepapers/real-time-analytics-109676.html
16.	15	2021 Digital Consumer Trends Index 16 March 2021: https://www.cheetahdigital.com/blog/2021-digital-consumer-trends-index/
17.	16	Over-thinking the Protection of Personal Information Act, by De Stadler, Hattingh, Esselaar & Boast. Juta 2021
18.	16	Principles of Data Protection: https://www.dataprotection.ie/en/individuals/data-protection-basics/principles-data-protection/

Reference Number	Chapter	
19.	17	Why Customer Experience Is Key for Loyalty Programs: 2 July 2018 https://sloanreview.mit.edu/article/why-customer-experience-is-key-for-loyalty-programs/
20.	18	Definition of 'loyalty': https://www.collinsdictionary.com/dictionary/english/loyalty
21.	18	Definition of 'promiscuous' https://www.dictionary.com/browse/promiscuous
22.	23	Dharmesh Bhana, Executive for Loyalty and Rewards Nedbank, Truth Leaders in Loyalty Summit 2021: https://truth.co.za/leaders-in-loyalty/dharmesh-bhana-nedbank/
23.	24	Liquid Barcodes #46: The Compelling Case for Coffee Subscriptions 25 October 2020: https://www.liquidbarcodes.com/podcasts/46-compelling-case-for-coffee-subscriptions/
24.	24	Pret's five-coffees-a-day subscription rises to £30 a month 26 April 2023: https://www.theguardian.com/business/2023/apr/26/pret-a-manger-subscription-rises-to-30-a-month-club-pret
25.	30	ebbo (formally known as Clarus Commerce): https://www.ebbo.com/
26.	33	Capgemini: https://www.capgemini.com/
27.	34	Let's Talk Loyalty #155 Dr Nejib Ben-Khedher, Head Emirates Skywards 28 October 2021: https://letstalkloyalty.com/155/
28.	35	Shop loyalty card data may help spot ovarian cancer by Michelle Roberts 27 January 2023: https://www.bbc.com/news/health-64411459
29.	36	RESCI, The Data-Driven Marketer's Guide to Lifecycle Marketing: https://www.retentionscience.com/
30.	39	How Customer Experience Drives Business Growth 6 June 2022: https://www.forrester.com/report/how-customer-experience-drives-business-growth-2022/RES177564
31.	40	Let's Talk Loyalty #383 Lindsay Eichten, Director of CRM Loyalty and Media TGI Fridays 24 May 2023: https://letstalkloyalty.com/383/
32.	44	The Future of Loyalty Report 2023: https://www.odu.edu/loyalty-science-lab/future-of-loyalty
33.	45	What Britons want from loyalty programmes 2.0: https://www.mando-connect.co.uk/what-brits-want-from-loyalty
34.	48	Bond Brand Loyalty: https://www.bondbrandloyalty.com/
35.	49	Pets At Home: https://cloud.digital.petsathome.com/vip
36.	50	Stephane Baschiera, ex CEO LVMH Moet Hennessy Louis Vuitton Inc
37.	51	2021 Loyalty Barometer Report : https://www.merkle.com/en/merkle-now/articles-blogs/2021/May/four-key-customer-insights-for-loyalty-and-rewards.html

Reference Number	Chapter	
38.	55	Andre Larisma, ex CEO Sanlam Reality - Leaders in Loyalty Summit 2019
39.	58	Len Llaguno, Founder and Managing Partner KYROS
40.	59	Jean Tranter, Head of Analytics The Foschini Group - Leaders in Loyalty Summit 2019
41.	60	Charlie Hills, Managing Director and Head of Strategy and Isobel Finlayson, Senior Account Director and Sustainability Lead Mando-Connect
42.	60	What the British want from Loyalty Programmes 3.0 2022: https://www.mando-connect.co.uk/what-the-british-want-from-loyalty-programmes-3/
43.	61	The Future of Loyalty Report 2023: https://www.odu.edu/loyalty-science-lab/future-of-loyalty
44.	62	Social and Behavioral Loyalty: https://www.annexcloud.com/social-loyalty
45.	63	The Future of Loyalty Report 2023: https://www.odu.edu/loyalty-science-lab/future-of-loyalty
46.	63	The Future of Loyalty Report 2023: https://www.odu.edu/loyalty-science-lab/future-of-loyalty
47.	65	Guy Rosenholz, CEO Nayax Coinbridge, Loyalty Magazine June 2023: https://www.internationalloyaltyawards.com/the-winners-edition-2023/
48.	65	The Loyalty Magazine June 2023: Payment Loyalty – Highly Commended in Best Loyalty Industry Innovation https://www.internationalloyaltyawards.com/the-winners-edition-2023/
49.	65	Let's Talk Loyalty #405 Ali Bin Zayed, Senior Manager Corporate Loyalty Emarat 13 July 2023: https://letstalkloyalty.com/405/
50.	66	Let's Talk Loyalty #326 Dr Melanie van Rooy, Head of Marketing Clicks 11 January 2023: https://letstalkloyalty.com/326/
51.	68	Pawel Dziadkowiec, former BP Loyalty Manager – article for Open Loyalty 2021:https://www.openloyalty.io/insider/loyalty-programs-in-fuel-retail
52.	69	Unlocking Direct-to-Consumer Relationships in CPG 2022: https://www.cheetahdigital.com/wp-content/uploads/2022_cd_unlocking_dtc_consumer_relationships_in_cpg_ebook.pdf
53.	70	Let's Talk Loyalty #374 Matt McLellan, VP Customer Planning and Proposition Asda 3 May 2023: https://letstalkloyalty.com/374/
54.	71	The Future of Fashion Retail 2023 Report – Comarch and The Loyalty People: https://www.comarch.com/trade-and-services/loyalty-marketing/news/the-future-of-fashion-retail-2023-comarch-and-the-loyalty-people-report-is-here/
55.	72	The Wise Marketer Women in Loyalty Episode 11 Kelly Mahoney, Vice President of Customer Marketing Ulta 13 May 2022: https://thewisemarketer.com/women-in-loyalty-episode-11-kelly-mahoney-ulta-beauty/
56.	73	Let's Talk Loyalty #375 David Parker, CEO of Polymath Consulting and Chair of the International Loyalty Awards Judging Panel 4 May 2023: https://letstalkloyalty.com/375/
57.	75	Let's Talk Loyalty #359 Mehdi Hemici, Chief Loyalty & eCommerce Officer Accor hotels 29 March 2023: https://letstalkloyalty.com/359/

Reference Number	Chapter	
58.	76	Let's Talk Loyalty #351 Rory Sutherland, Vice Chairman Ogilvy Group 9 March 2023: https://letstalkloyalty.com/351/
59.	76	Rupert Hogg, CEO Cathay Pacific – Bloomberg 18 March 2019: https://www.bloomberg.com/news/articles/2019-03-18/cathay-will-mine-personal-data-to-tailor-business-class-service#xj4y7vzkg
60.	76	Let's Talk Loyalty #408 Dr Nejib Ben-Kheder, Head Emirates Skywards 20 July 2023: https://letstalkloyalty.com/408/
61.	84	Richard Dutton, Managing Director of Elias Partnership
62.	84	How loyalty programs are helping to solve privacy concerns in a cookieless world – YouGov 3 April 2021: https://today.yougov.com/topics/consumer/articles-reports/2021/05/03/loyalty-programs-privacy-cookieless-world-poll
63.	84	What are the Differences Between Anonymisation and Pseudonymisation 3 June 2023: https://www.privacycompany.eu/blogpost-en/what-are-the-differences-between-anonymisation-and-pseudonymisation
64.	85	Loyalty Fraud Prevention: https://www.comarch.com/artificial-intelligence-management/loyalty-fraud-prevention/
65.	86	Detecting and Preventing Loyalty Fraud: Technology Explained 16 June 2022: https://antavo.com/blog/fraud-detection-in-loyalty-programs/
66.	93	Here's how major loyalty programs make hundreds of millions of dollars profit 27 May 2020: https://loyaltyrewardco.com/heres-how-major-loyalty-programs-make-hundreds-of-millions-of-dollars-profit/
67.	96	Motista: https://www.motista.com/
68.	97	2022 Experience Trends Report: Four Trends That Are Changing Customer & Employee Experiences This Year: https://inmoment.com/en-gb/resource/2022-experience-trends-report/
69.	97	It Pays To Share: Refer-A-Friend Programs Boost Customer Acquisition And Engagement 7 March 2023: https://www.forrester.com/blogs/refer-a-friend-programs-boost-customer-acquisition/
70.	97	Why Customer Referrals Can Drive Stunning Profits June 2011: https://hbr.org/2011/06/why-customer-referrals-can-drive-stunning-profits
71.	97	The Future of Customer Loyalty in 2023 & Beyond: https://www.annexcloud.com/resources/guides/the-future-of-customer-loyalty-in-2023-beyond/
72.	98	Let's Talk Loyalty #293 Andrew Francis, Value Stream Owner Residential Genesis 26 October 2022: https://letstalkloyalty.com/293/
73.	99	https://www.customerstrategynetwork.com/
74.	99	Let's Talk Loyalty #122 and #308 Yuping Liu-Thompkins, Founder and Director of the Loyalty Science Lab 8 July 2019 and 30 November 2022: https://letstalkloyalty.com/122/ and https://letstalkloyalty.com/308/
75.	99	The Secret to Loyalty? Make Customers Feel Like They Belong 6 January 2023: https://loyaltyrewardco.com/the-secret-to-loyalty-make-customers-feel-like-they-belong/

Contributors

My sincere thanks to our contributors:

Chapter

14 Dr Shorful Islam, CEO Be Data Solutions
https://bedatasolutions.com/

22 Iain Pringle, Managing Partner New World Loyalty
https://newworldloyalty.com/

23 David Slavick, Partner and Co-Founder Ascendant Loyalty
https://ascendantloyalty.com/

30 Truth and BrandMapp Loyalty Whitepaper
https://truth.co.za/articles/whitepapers/

40 Pavel Los, Customer Engagement and Loyalty Strategy Director Oracle CrowdTwist
https://www.oracle.com/za/cx/marketing/customer-loyalty/

49 Cecilia Floridi, Managing Director DataLab
https://www.datalab-crm.de/

54 The Loyalty Podcast
https://podcasts.apple.com/bh/podcast/loyalty-podcast/id1478145967

60 Charlie Hills, MD and Head of Strategy Mando-Connect
https://www.mando-connect.co.uk/

64 Glenn Gillis, CEO and Co-Founder Sea Monster
https://www.seamonster.co.za/

69 Sadika Fakir, Group Executive: Digital Marketing and Media Absa
Former Integrated Media and Digital Director, Tiger Brands

70 Melissa Hanley, Head of Marketing Pick n Pay
https://www.pnp.co.za/

73 Johan Moolman, former CEO eBucks Rewards FNB
https://www.ebucks.com/web/eBucks/

74 Mateboho Malope, Group Loyalty Executive Vodacom
https://www.vodacom.co.za/

76 Rob McDonald, Chief Commercial Officer IAG Loyalty
https://www.iagloyalty.com/

77 Evert de Boer, Managing Partner On Point Loyalty and CEO Fidivio
https://onpointloyalty.com/

78 Ros Netto, Head of Loyalty Kauai and Virgin Active SA
https://kauai.co.za/, https://www.virginactive.co.za/

79 Celeste Williams, Head of Marketing SA Discovery Vitality
https://www.discovery.co.za/

80 Mark Maclure, Founding Director Stream Loyalty
https://streamloyalty.com/

85 & 86 Loyalty Fraud Group: Willem Strydom (Old Mutual), Ros Netto (Kauai/Virgin Active SA), Yunus Patel (Virgin Active SA), Francois Slabbert (Discovery SA), Carla Pullen (Cape Union Mart), Belinda Brink (Clicks Group), Leanne Oosthuizen (Gratifii)

89 Charles Ehredt, CEO Currency Alliance
https://www.currencyalliance.com/

95 Len Llaguno, Founder and Managing Partner KYROS
https://www.kyros.com/

BLIND

LOYALTY

The Blind Loyalty Trust

Thank you for buying and reading *Blind Loyalty*. All profits generated by this book go to The Blind Loyalty Trust.

The Trust's purpose is to offer hope and clarity to underprivileged patients requiring critical corneal transplant surgery. Founder Amanda Cromhout says, "Being sight-impaired has been the biggest life adjustment I have faced in 52 years, not to mention the three months of terrifying pain in 2022. The Blind Loyalty Trust can help less fortunate patients requiring similar eye-saving surgery."

How can the loyalty industry support the trust globally?

1. Buy *Blind Loyalty* for your friends and colleagues – share the loyalty love.
2. If you run a loyalty programme, please consider activating the redemption of points to The Blind Loyalty Trust.
3. We sell beautifully crafted Blind Loyalty bracelets to generate profits for the trust. If you are a retailer wishing to resell or an organisation wishing to offer conference or year-end gifts, this is the perfect opportunity to help others.
4. Donate generously as an individual or as a corporate.

For all queries, donations to the trust, and to see the *Blind Loyalty* bracelets, please visit www.blindloyaltytrust.com

truth.
CUSTOMER. LEADERSHIP

WELCOME

TO THE HOME OF LOYALTY.

Amanda Cromhout is the Founder and CEO of Truth. Truth provides you with a one-stop solution for everything in your world of loyalty. From strategy and programme design to member engagement and loyalty KPIs, we are here to serve your every loyalty requirement.

STRATEGY

The team at Truth has a wealth of experience in creating and executing world-class loyalty customer strategies for our clients. Our 'customer leadership' spans from loyalty programme design/re-design through to customer centricity at the core of your business.

CUSTOMER ACADEMY

Six weeks to your next level of loyalty brilliance! The Truth Customer Academy online loyalty course is fully accredited globally for certified professional development. Join the hundreds of other loyalty professionals who have taken their career to the next level with the Truth online loyalty course.

KEYNOTE SPEAKING

Amanda Cromhout is a sought-after keynote speaker who offers insight and inspiration to any corporate or loyalty event. Her topics cover loyalty leadership, putting the customer first, and her inspirational story behind *Blind Loyalty.*

"Rated best speaker, not once, twice, thrice, but four times at our conferences..."

Please email amanda@truth.co.za or visit www.amandacromhout.com / www.truth.co.za

First published in South Africa in 2023.

ISBN: 978-0-7961-1175-3

Made in the USA
Middletown, DE
28 December 2024

68306200R00137